SCIENCE WORKSHOP SERIES

EARTH SCIENCE

Oceans and Atmosphere

Seymour Rosen

GLOBE BOOK COMPANY
A Division of Simon & Schuster
Paramus, New Jersey

THE AUTHOR

Seymour Rosen received his B.A. and M.S. degrees from Brooklyn College. He taught science in the New York City School System for twenty-seven years. Mr. Rosen was also a contributing participant in a teacher-training program for the development of science curriculum for the New York City Board of Education.

Cover Photograph: NASA
Photo Researcher: Rhoda Sidney

ISBN: 0-8359-0385-0

Printed in the United States of America
   8 9 10 11   00 99 98 97

GLOBE BOOK COMPANY
A Division of Simon & Schuster
Paramus, New Jersey

CONTENTS

WEATHER

Introduction to Oceans and Atmosphere

Have you ever gone to a ball game or to an outdoor concert only to get "rained out?" Have you ever listened to the radio to find out if heavy snow has closed your school?

Weather affects all of our lives. A weather report may have helped you decide how to dress this morning. In this book, you will find out why winds blow and how raindrops form. You will become an expert on reading weather maps, and learn how to make them yourself. You will learn many things about the air that surrounds the earth.

In this book, you also will learn about the vast oceans that cover three-quarters of the earth's surface. You will learn about ocean waves, why the ocean is important, and how the oceans benefit you.

In addition, you will learn about air and water pollution and what you can do the help control the problem and save the environment.

What is the hydrosphere? | 1

hydrosphere [HY-droh-sfeer]:   water part of our planet
ocean currents: streams of water flowing in the ocean

LESSON 1 | What is the hydrosphere?

Have you ever seen pictures of the earth taken from space? You can see clouds, land, and water. In fact, you see <u>mostly</u> water. That is why the earth is sometimes called the "water planet." Only 29 percent of the earth's surface is land. The rest – 71 percent – is water. We call the water part of our planet the **hydrosphere** [HY-droh-sfeer].

The hydrosphere includes all of the salt water and fresh water on the earth. Salt water makes up about 97 percent of all the water on the earth. Most of the salt water is in the world ocean. Fresh water is found in rivers, lakes, and streams. However, most of the fresh water on the earth is frozen in ice.

The world ocean makes up most of the hydrosphere. But we think of it as three major oceans. They are the Atlantic, Pacific, and Indian Oceans. We also use the names Arctic Ocean and Antarctic Ocean for areas of the Atlantic and Pacific Oceans.

The Pacific Ocean covers the largest area of the world ocean. More than half of the earth's ocean water is in the Pacific. It is also the world's deepest ocean. The Atlantic Ocean is the second largest ocean. The Indian Ocean is the smallest.

The oceans are all connected, but the waters move as if they were several separate bodies. These separate movements are called **ocean currents.** Currents have been called "rivers of water" in the ocean.

You will learn more about ocean currents on the facing page.

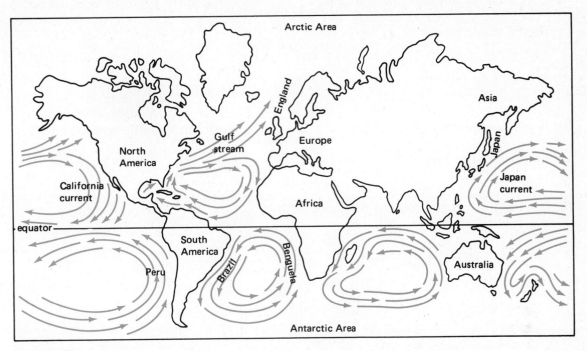

Figure A

Figure A shows the major ocean currents. Notice their circular paths. Each one covers a great distance.

What causes ocean currents?

- Global winds are the chief cause of currents.

- The spinning of the earth causes currents to move at an angle.

- The continents (land) cause currents to turn.

The ocean currents can be <u>warm</u> or <u>cold</u>. Currents that flow from the equator are warm currents. Currents that come from the North Pole and South Pole are cold currents.

Use Figure A to answer these questions.

1. North of the equator, the ocean currrents move in a _____ direction.

clockwise, counterclockwise

2. South of the equator, the ocean currents move in a _____ direction.

clockwise, counterclockwise

Follow the path of the Gulf Stream.

3. The Gulf Stream starts in the Gulf of Mexico where the water is _____ .

warm, cold

4. The Gulf Stream flows _____ toward Europe.

northeast, southwest

5. It flows toward the coast of _____ .

Japan, England

Which current?

6. If you tossed a bottle into the _____ Ocean it could be washed up
   Pacific, Atlantic

   on the coast of Japan.

7. It would be carried toward Japan by the _____ current.
   Gulf Stream, Japan

8. If you tossed a bottle into the _____ Ocean it could be washed up
   Pacific, Atlantic

   on the coast of England.

9. It would be carried toward England by the _____ current.
   Gulf Stream, California

10. The ocean currents near Brazil are _____ .
    warm , cold

OCEAN CURRENTS AFFECT CLIMATE

The oceans and the atmosphere work together in many ways. Air masses pick up water over oceans and bring rain to the land. But ocean currents also affect climate.

For example, the Gulf Stream starts in a warm part of the earth. Gulf Stream water is warmer than the water next to it. Winds that blow over the Gulf Stream pick up some of this warmth and moisture. The warm, moist air blowing over the Gulf Stream brings mild weather with it.

Figure B

London is famous for its "pea soup" fogs. They form when warm Gulf Stream water meets colder water off the English Coast.

Figure C

Imagine that you are a ship's captain.

1. If you were sailing to England from the United States, you would _____ the Gulf Stream.
<small>seek out, avoid</small>

2. Why? _____

   _____

3. If you were sailing from England to the United States you would _____ the Gulf Stream.
<small>seek out, avoid</small>

4. Why? _____

   _____

WORD SCRAMBLE

Below are several scrambled words you have used in this Lesson. Unscramble the words and write your answers in the spaces provided.

1. RUCTERN   _____

2. SEERPHOHRDY   _____

3. TINNONECT   _____

4. NOCEA   _____

5. PCICFIA   _____

Complete each statement using a term or terms from the list below. Write your answers in the spaces provided.

continent	cold currents	equator
warm currents	ocean currents	global winds
move at an angle	poles	clockwise

1. The general movements of the ocean waters are called _____ .

2. The chief cause of ocean currents is the _____ .

3. The turning of the earth makes the currents _____ .

4. An ocean current turns around when it comes near a _____ .

5. In the part of the world you live, the ocean currents move in a _____ direction.

6. Ocean currents are classified as _____ and _____ .

7. Warm currents start near the _____ .

8. Cold currents start near the _____ .

Use Figure D to answer the questions.

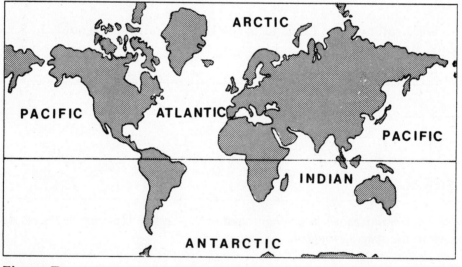

Figure D

Most of the earth's water is part of one huge ocean. But it has been divided into three major oceans.

1. Name the oceans. _____

2. Which is the largest ocean? _____

3. What other names do we use for areas of the Atlantic and Pacific Oceans? _____

_____

Where does rainwater go? 2

ground water: water that collects in pores in the soil

LESSON 2 | Where does rainwater go?

It rains on almost all places of our Earth. You have probably seen both heavy rains and light rains. Did you ever think about where the rain water goes?

You probably know part of the answer to this question. Rain falls into oceans, lakes, rivers, and steams. It becomes part of our surface water. Surface water can be seen on the surface of the earth.

However, some rainwater also seeps into the ground. It is **ground water**. Ground water is under the surface of the earth. The ground water is just below the surface of the ground. In other places it is very far below the surface—hundreds of meters (thousands of feet).

The ground water seeps into the ground until it rests on solid rock. Then it cannot seep farther. The water builds up similar to water filling a bathtub. It gets higher and higher. The level of the top of ground water is called the water table.

The water table keeps changing. It is higher when there is lots of rain. It is lower when there is no rain—or little rain.

We do not often see ground water, but it is important. People dig wells and get drinking water from ground water. Plants get water through their roots from ground water.

Lakes may be formed from ground water. Where the land dips below the water table, a lake forms. If the land dips only slightly below the water table, a swamp forms.

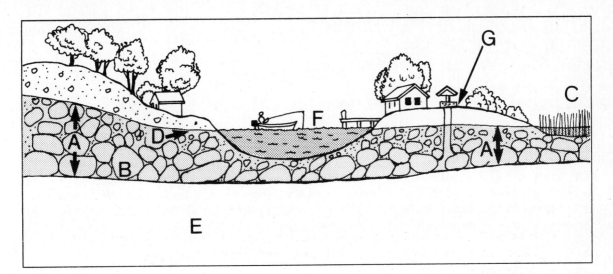

Figure A

1. Identify the following by letter.

   a) water table _____

   b) swamp _____

   c) lake _____

   d) well _____

   e) solid rock _____

   f) solid-rock line _____

   g) crust below the surface that is soaked with water _____

2. Trace the water table (line) with a red pencil.

3. The water table _____ a straight line.

is, is not

4. A water table _____ change.

does, does not

5. When there is little rain . . .

   a) the water table _____ .

rises, lowers

   b) the lake level _____ .

rises, lowers

   c) the swamp water _____ .

rises, may dry out

   d) the well water _____ .

rises, may dry out

6. When there is a lot of rain . . .

    a) the water table _____ .
                           rises, lowers

    b) the lake level _____ .
                          rises, lowers

    c) the swamp water _____ .
                           rises, may dry out

    d) the well water level _____ .
                           rises, may dry out

The kind of soil a place has also affects the water table. Some places have tightly packed soil, or soil that has a lot of clay in it. Clay and tight soil hold back water. It cannot seep into the ground. Usually, these places have low water tables. Soil that is good for crops and holding water has many holes in it and very little clay.

FILL IN THE BLANK

Complete each statement using a term or terms from the list below. Write your answers in the spaces provided.

far below	surface water	high
lakes	swamps	water table
ground water	low	amount of rainfall
always changing	near	drinking water
water to plants		

1. Water on the ground is called _____ .

2. Water that is below the earth's surface is called _____ .

3. The upper level of ground water is called the _____ .

4. In some places the water table is _____ . In other places it is

    _____ .

5. _____ and _____ form in places where the land dips

    below the water table.

6. The water table is _____ .

7. The water table is affected by the _____ .

8. In dry climates, the water table is _____ the surface.

9. In wet climates, the water table is usually _____ the surface.

10. Ground water is important because it gives _____ and

    _____ .

MATCHING

Match each term in Column A with its description in Column B. Write the correct letter in the space provided.

	Column A		Column B
_____	1. water table	a)	has high water table
_____	2. swamp area	b)	lowers the water table
_____	3. heavy rainfall	c)	lakes and streams
_____	4. dry period	d)	upper level of ground water
_____	5. surface water	e)	raises the water table

TRUE OR FALSE

In the space provided, write "true" if the sentence is true. Write "false" if the sentence is false.

_____ 1. The water table is mostly underground.

_____ 2. The water table is the same everywhere.

_____ 3. The water table changes.

_____ 4. During dry weather, the water table rises.

_____ 5. During wet weather, the water table rises.

_____ 6. Swamps are found in places that have a high water table.

_____ 7. A lake can dry up.

_____ 8. Much rain always means a high water table.

_____ 9. Good soil has a lot of clay.

_____ 10. Ground water is important only to plants.

Use the clues to complete the crossword puzzle.

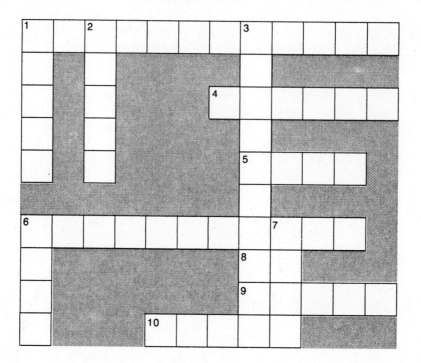

CLUES

Across

1. Water you can see on the surface of the earth.

4. River.

5. It falls into streams.

6. Water that is under the surface of the earth.

8. Where land dips below the water table there may _____ a lake.

9. Bodies of water surrounded by land.

10. When there is little rain, the water table is _____ .

Down

1. If the land dips a little below the water table, there is a _____ .

2. Very wide stream.

3. The level of the top of ground water.

6. Ground water is _____ for plants.

7. "Raindrop" from your eye.

How do scientists explore the ocean?

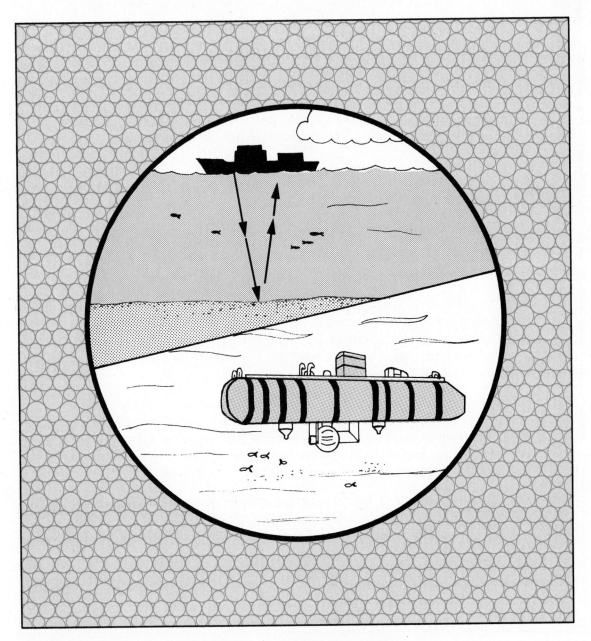

oceanography [oh-shun-OG-ruh-fee]: study of the oceans
submersibles [sub-MUR-suh-bulz]: underwater research vessel

LESSON 3 | How do scientists explore the ocean?

Powerful! Mysterious! Frightening! Awesome! Beautiful! Fascinating! These are but a few of the terms used to describe the ocean. Were you ever on the ocean? Did you ever watch — and hear ocean waves crashing onto shore? How would you describe the ocean?

Over the ages, people wondered about the ocean. They wanted to find the answers to many questions — such as: How deep is the ocean? What does the ocean floor look like? What kinds of life exist in deep water? What causes waves, tides, and currents? And, do sea monsters really exist?

People have always wanted to explore the ocean floor. But two things have made this exploration very difficult:

1) People cannot breathe in water.

2) Water pressure is very great deep down in the ocean. It can easily crush a person.

Special equipment has been built. It lets scientists safely explore thousands of meters below the waves. For example, in 1943 the Aqua-Lung (SCUBA) was invented. Scuba equipment cannot be used in deep water. Yet, it was an important breakthrough. It continues to be used widely for hobby and scientific underwater activity.

Scientists can study the ocean floor by drilling into the crust beneath the ocean. The research ship *Glomar Challenger* was specially built for an ocean research program called the Deep Sea Drilling Project. Equipment on the ship can drill more than 4 km below the surface. Scientists study samples of rock taken from the ocean floor.

Scientists also use underwater vessels to explore the oceans. These vessels are called **submersibles** [sub-MUR-suh-bulz]. One kind of submersible is lowered into the ocean on a steel cable from a ship. Another kind is a small submarine. Scientists have discovered many unusual living things deep in the ocean while in submersibles.

Ocean study is called **oceanography** (oh-shun-OG-ruh-fee). The first ocean-going research expedition was made by the *H.M.S. Challenger*. This British vessel cast off from Portsmouth, England on December 21, 1872.

It cruised for 727 days, and covered nearly 70 thousand miles. During that time, scientists recorded numerous observations, and carried out many experiments. They also collected sea floor sediment and nearly 5000 kinds of plants and animals never seen before.

The Challenger's voyage marked the birth of oceanography.

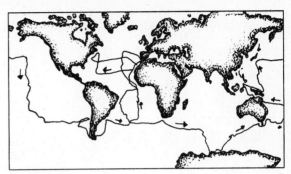

Figure A

MORE ABOUT SUBMERSIBLES

The most advanced and useful submersible is the *Alvin*. The Navy owns *Alvin*. But it is operated by a private ocean-research organization.

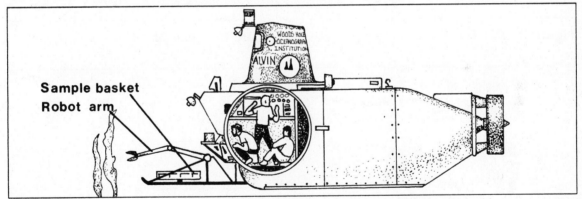

Sample basket
Robot arm

Figure B   *Alvin*

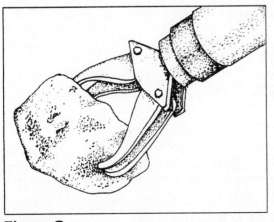

Figure C

Alvin is pressurized, and can move about freely on the ocean floor. It carries its own oxygen. *Alvin* has a robot arm. It can grab things and assist in experiments. *Alvin* can descend as far as 13,000 feet. That's more than two miles. *Alvin* is shown in Figure B with a "full house". How many persons can

Alvin hold? _____

The pictures below show many of the vessels and instruments used to study the ocean.

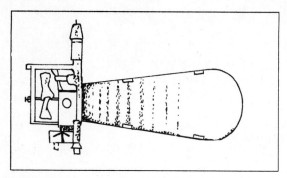

Figure D   *Deep water current detector*

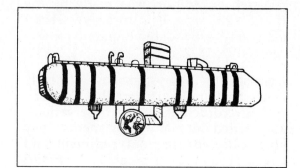

Figure E   *Bathyscaphe*

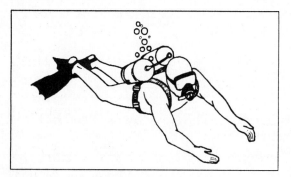

Figure F   *SCUBA*

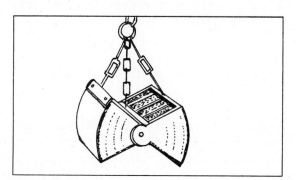

Figure G   *Grab bucket*

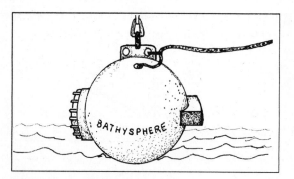

Figure H   *Bathysphere*

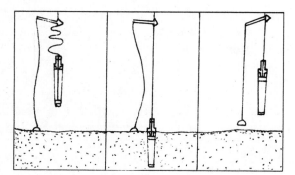

Figure I   *Coring tube*

Figure J   *Early diving suit*

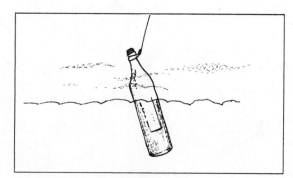

Figure K   *Drift bottle*

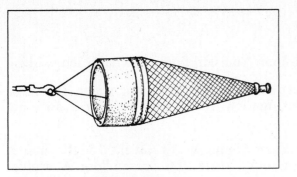

Figure L *Plankton townet*

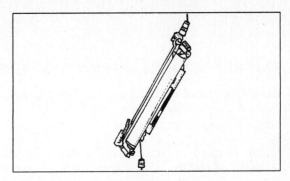

Figure M *Nansen bottle*

Study Figures D to M. Then match the "tools" with their descriptions. Write their names on the spaces provided.

_____

1. Cone-shaped cloth bag held open by a metal ring. It catches tiny marine organisms as it is towed slowly behind a ship.

_____

2. Just a closed waterproof container with a note in it. It is carried along by the ocean currents. The note asks that anyone who find the bottle return it indicating where it was found. In this way, scientists trace ocean currents.

_____

3. Shaped like an open clam. When it touches the bottom, the halves snap shut. As it shuts, it takes along sea floor samples.

_____

4. Shaped like a bomb. It is lowered into the ocean where it records currents far below the surface.

_____

5. Long and slim; double-side-by-side tubes. Collects water at any depth and records its temperature.

_____

6. A hollow tube that is forced into the ocean floor. The core fills with sea floor material.

_____

7. Completely self-contained. Diver moves freely without outside power.

_____

8. Bulky and heavy. Supplied oxygen from the surface. Lowered and lifted by rope that also limits diver's movements.

_____

9. Round vessel with heavy, thick steel walls. Lowered and raised by heavy steel cables. Pressurized. Carries one scientist.

_____

10. Looks like a fat submarine with a sphere connected to its underside. Carries two scientists. Pressurized. Propellers permit horizontal movement only.

In Lesson 5, you will learn about the ocean floor. You will find out what it looks like.

Scientists have learned a lot about the surface of the ocean floor using <u>sonar</u>. The word "sonar" comes from the letters in **Sound Navigation And Ranging**. Sonar is an echo-sounding system.

Sonar is used to figure out the depth of the ocean. Sound waves travel through water at a speed of 1500m/sec. A transmitter bounces a sound wave off the ocean floor. A receiver picks up the echo.

Scientists measure the time it takes for the echo to return. Let us say a sound wave makes it from the transmitter to the receiver in 10 seconds. The sound wave takes 5 seconds to reach the bottom and 5 seconds to return. Therefore, the depth of the ocean floor is 7500 m (1500m/sec X 5 sec).

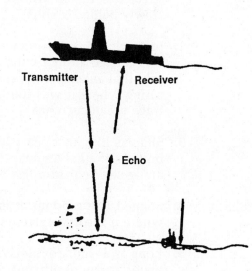

Figure N

REACHING OUT

Complete the chart below. The first column shows the amount of time it takes for a sound wave to make a round trip using SONAR. For each time, give the depth of the ocean floor in meters (m)

	Length of time(s)	Depth (meters)
1.	2 sec	
2.	6 sec	
3.	12 sec	

What are ocean waves? 4

crest: highest point of a wave
trough [TROFF]: lowest point of a wave
wave: regular up-and-down movement of water
wavelength: distance from one crest to the next crest

LESSON 4 | What are ocean waves?

What happens when you throw a pebble into still water? You see larger and larger rings moving outward from the center. They are **waves**. Waves transfer <u>energy</u> from one point to another.

The waves caused by the pebble are the same as <u>ocean</u> waves — only smaller — MUCH smaller.

A wave is the regular up-and-down movement of water. Some waves are caused by tides; some by earthquakes. Most waves, however, are caused by <u>wind</u> blowing across the water.

Wave size depends upon three things:

- wind s<u>peed</u>
- <u>how long</u> the wind blows — and
- the <u>fetch</u> or <u>how far</u> the wind blows across the ocean

A water wave has two main parts —

- a high point called the **crest** and
- a low point called the **trough** [TROFF].

- The distance between side-by-side crests — or side-by-side troughs is called the **wavelength**.

  - The distance between the crest and its trough is the wave height.
  - Many connected waves are called a wave train.

You can see the parts of a wave in Figure A on the next page.

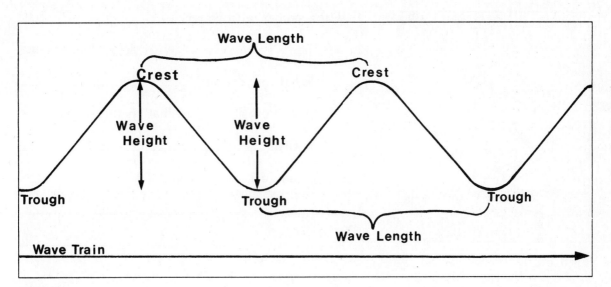

Figure A

1. In Figure B, identify the parts indicated by letter. Write the correct name next to the letter.

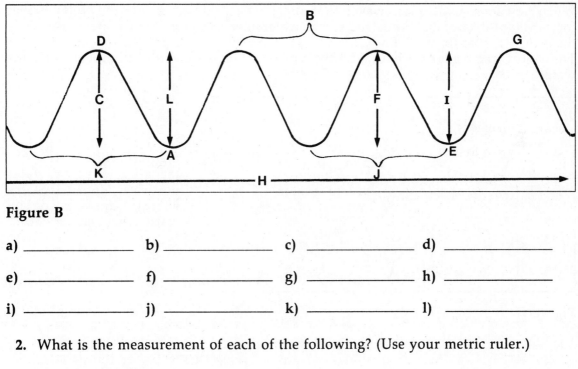

Figure B

a) _____ b) _____ c) _____ d) _____

e) _____ f) _____ g) _____ h) _____

i) _____ j) _____ k) _____ l) _____

2. What is the measurement of each of the following? (Use your metric ruler.)

   a) wave <u>height</u> _____ mm

   b) wave <u>length</u> _____ mm

3. a) Are all the waves of this wave train the same size? _____

   b) Take a guess — <u>Must</u> all the waves of a given wave train be the same size?

   _____

21

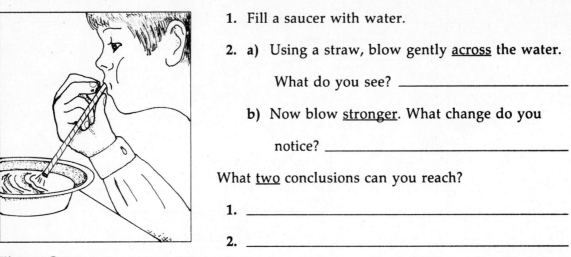

1. Fill a saucer with water.

2. a) Using a straw, blow gently <u>across</u> the water.

   What do you see? _____

   b) Now blow <u>stronger</u>. What change do you

   notice? _____

What <u>two</u> conclusions can you reach?

   1. _____

   2. _____

Figure C

UNDERSTANDING HOW OCEAN WATER MOVES

When you look at deep-sea waves (not shore waves) it seems that the water moves forward rapidly. But that is not true. Ocean water moves in a series of circular paths. Only the energy moves forward. Energy is passed along from water particle to water particle. The energy transfer is enormous. BUT there is surprisingly little forward movement of the water.

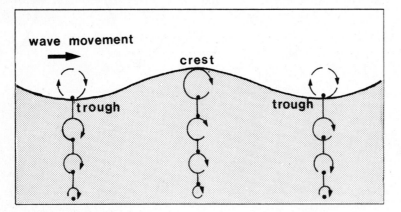

Figure D shows the circular movement of water particles. Notice that the energy transfer is <u>downward</u> as well as forward.

Figure D

1. As you go deeper, the energy circles become _____ .
   larger, smaller

2. This means that energy transfer _____ the deeper you go.
   increases, decreases

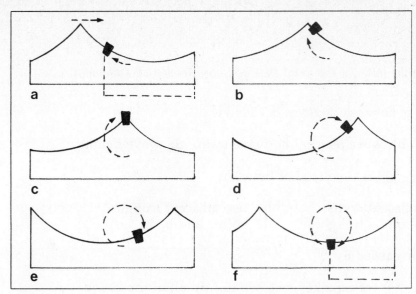

You can see the movement of water by watching a floating cork. Figure E shows a cork "riding the waves."

You can see that as a wave moves by, the cork moves slightly forward. But then it falls back as the wave passes.

Figure E

3. The cork moves with the water. If the water itself were moving forward rapidly, the cork would _____ .
   stay in the same place, move to the right

4. Compared to the starting position "a", the cork in "f" has moved

   _____ .
   only slightly forward, to the far right

5. This shows that the water, itself, _____ moved forward very far.
   has, has not

TIME FOR A BREAK(ER)!

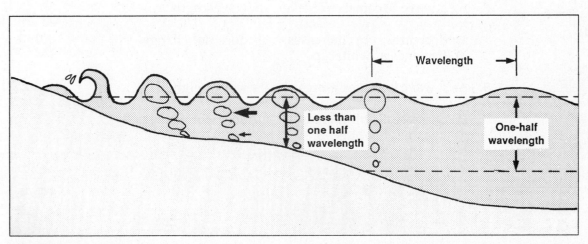

Figure F

As waves move toward the shore, the trough of each wave touches the ocean bottom. Friction slows down the wave. The top, or crest, keeps moving at the same speed. It gets farther and farther ahead of the trough. Finally, it falls over and forms a breaker.

MULTIPLE CHOICE

In the space provided, write the letter of the word that best completes each statement.

_____ 1. A group of connected waves is called a

   a) crest **b)** wave length **c)** wave train **d)** wave height

_____ 2. A wave <u>height</u> is the distance between

   a) two adjacent crests.   **b)** two adjacent troughs.
   c) a crest and a trough.   **d)** both a and b.

_____ 3. Waves are caused by

   a) tides. **b)** earthquakes. **c)** wind. **d)** all of the above.

_____ 4. <u>Most</u> waves are caused by

   a) tides. **b)** earthquakes. **c)** wind. **d)** volcanoes.

_____ 5. The distance wind blows over water is called its

   a) wavelength **b)** fetch. **c)** mileage. **d)** swell.

_____ 6. A <u>wavelength</u> is the distance between

   a) two adjacent crests.   **b)** two adjacent troughs.
   c) a crest and a trough.   **d)** both a and b.

_____ 7. Wave size is affected by

   a) wind speed. **b)** fetch. **c)** time wind lasts. **d)** all of the above.

_____ 8. As a wave becomes a breaker, its wavelength

   a) decreases. **b)** increases. **c)** does not change.
   d) becomes a whitecap.

_____ 9. As a wave becomes a breaker, its wave <u>height</u>

   a) decreases. **b)** increases. **c)** does not change.
   d) becomes a whitecap.

What does the ocean floor look like?

continental shelf: part of a continent that slopes gently away from the shoreline
continental slope: part of a continent between the continental shelf and the ocean floor
mid-ocean ridge: underwater mountain range

LESSON 5 | What does the ocean floor look like?

Most of the earth's water is found in our oceans. The oceans lie in huge basins. But the water spreads beyond the basins. It goes onto low parts of the continents. The part of a continent that is covered by the ocean is called the **continental shelf**. The continental shelf slopes gradually downward.

At the end of the continental shelf, the ocean floor drops sharply. This sharp drop is called the **continental slope**.

The basin begins at the bottom of the continental slope. The average depth of the deep-sea basin is 426 meters (1400 feet).

If all the ocean water would suddenly disappear, what would you see? You would see many of the features found on land.

The ocean floor has flat areas. It also has high mountains, volcanoes and deep canyons.

- The flat areas are called plains.

- Ranges of mountains that run through the middle of the ocean are called **mid-ocean ridges.** In some places, mid-ocean ridges rise above the ocean surface. They form islands.

- Volcanoes are scattered on the ocean floor. Some underwater volcanoes reach above the ocean surface. They form volcanic islands. The Hawaiian Islands are the peaks of underwater volcanoes.

- Submarine canyons are long valleys with steep sides. They are found along the continental shelf.

- The deepest parts of the ocean are called trenches. Most trenches are near chains of volcanic islands that are close to a continent.

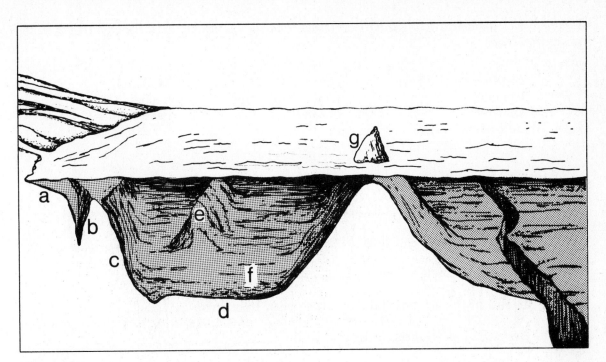

Figure A

Figure A shows features of the ocean floor. They are listed below. Identify each feature by writing the correct letter in the spaces provided.

1. continental shelf _____

2. continental slope _____

3. deep sea basin _____

4. volcanic mountain _____

5. submarine canyon _____

6. mid-ocean ridge _____

7. plain _____

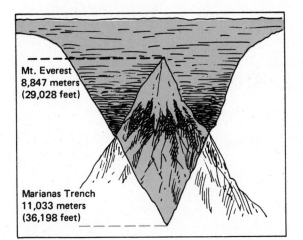

Figure B

Trenches are the deepest parts of our planet.

The deepest trench is the Marianas Trench in the Pacific. It reaches down 11,033 meters (36,198 feet).

Mount Everest is the earth's tallest mountain. The Marianas Trench is deeper than Mount Everest is high.

If Mount Everest were placed into the Marianas Trench, how many meters of water would be above its peak?

FILL IN THE BLANK

Complete each statement using a term or terms from the list below. Write your answers in the spaces provided.

> continental shelf   submarine   Marianas
> trenches   continental slope basins
> sharply   oceans   gradually
> mid-ocean ridges

1. Most of the earth's water is found in the _____ .

2. The oceans lie in huge _____ .

3. The part of the continent that is under the ocean is called the _____ .

4. The continental shelf slants _____ .

5. At the end of the continental slope the ocean floor drop _____ .

6. The deep-sea basin starts at the end of the _____ .

7. Mountain ranges in the ocean are called _____ .

8. Valleys in the continental shelf are called _____ canyons.

9. The deepest places along the ocean floor are _____ .

10. The deepest trench in the world is the _____ Trench.

MATCHING

Match each term in Column A with its description in Column B. Write the correct letter in the space provided.

Column A	Column B
_____ 1. water planet	a) underwater mountain ranges
_____ 2. continental shelf	b) deepest part of the earth
_____ 3. plain	c) flat area
_____ 4. trench	d) low part of a continent covered by the ocean
_____ 5. mid-ocean ridges	e) earth

TRUE OR FALSE

In the space provided, write "true" if the sentence is true. Write "false" if the sentence is false.

_____ 1. The earth is the only planet.

_____ 2. Only our planet has a lot of water.

_____ 3. The earth's water layer is called the atmosphere.

_____ 4. The continental shelf has a gentle slant.

_____ 5. The continental slope has a gentle slant.

_____ 6. The deep sea floor starts at the beginning of the continental shelf.

_____ 7. A ridge is a high place on the ocean floor.

_____ 8. A submarine canyon is a low place on the ocean floor.

_____ 9. A submarine canyon is deeper than a trench.

_____ 10. The ocean floor has some flat places.

REACHING OUT

In the space below, draw a model of the ocean floor that shows each of the following: continental shelf, continental slope, mid-ocean ridge, plains, trenches, submarine canyon, underwater volcano.

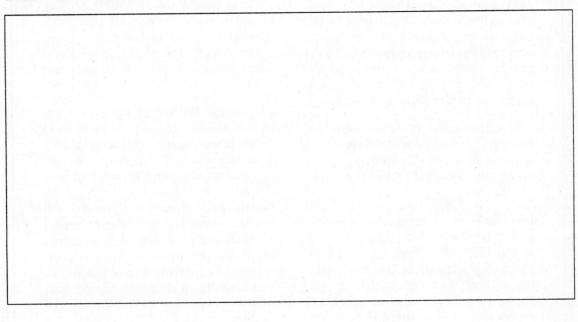

SCIENCE *EXTRA*

Offshore Oil

Can you imagine a structure taller than Chicago's Sears Tower, the tallest building in the world, rising from the ocean floor? Like a giant iceberg, only a small part of the structure is above the water. The rest is found underwater. These giant sea structures do exist. And even taller ones are planned. They are the products of a new geologic frontier—deep water oil exploration and recovery.

The uses of oil in modern society are constantly increasing. However, the sources of oil are decreasing. As a result, the search for new oil sources continues.

Most known oil reserves are found on land. However, it was discovered in the 1930s that there are vast supplies of oil found below the continental shelf. Some geologists believe there may be nearly as much oil under the shelf as there is on land.

Offshore drilling is oil drilling in shallow water, done close to shore. There are several important offshore drilling areas in the United States. For example, the Gulf of Mexico, off the shore of Louisiana. Unfortunately, most of the easy-to-recover offshore reserves have been used up. The oil companies are aware of the decreasing supply of oil. Since 1984, they have been searching for new sources of oil in the deeper waters of the ocean.

Recovering oil from such depths is no easy task. Shallow water drilling is done from permanent platforms attached to the ocean floor. Deep water "rigs" are much more complex; more complex to design and construct.

In general, the larger structures are not as stable. They must be able to withstand hurricane winds and crushing waves. Deep-sea ocean rigs are mounted over the water above the continental shelf. Some are on floating platforms. Others are on platforms resting on the continental shelf. Because of the risk and cost involved, the entire venture of deep water oil exploration and discovery can only be undertaken by companies who are able to risk billions of dollars.

Why are the oceans important?

phytoplankton [fite-uh-PLANK-tun]: floating plants

LESSON 6 | Why are the oceans important?

The oceans are more important than you may think. Without the oceans, there would probably be no life on Earth. The oceans and the atmosphere work together to support living things.

Living things must breathe oxygen. This oxygen comes from green plants. Green plants that grow on land supply some oxygen to the air but only a small amount. Most of the oxygen of the air—about 90 percent—comes from microscopic sea plants and algae called **phytoplankton** [fite-uh-PLANK-tun]. Phytoplankton float near the surface of the ocean. Phytoplankton also supply oxygen to ocean water. Sea animals, as well as sea plants, use this oxygen.

There is another way in which the oceans and the atmosphere work together. Water evaporates from the oceans to form clouds. The clouds move over land. The moisture leaves the clouds in the form of rain or snow. Then, the plants and animals get the water they need. And, in some places, people depend upon ocean water to drink. But first, salts and other minerals in the water are removed at big plants.

The oceans are important in other ways too.

The oceans give us food. Fish and shellfish are two important foods we get from the seas. Millions of people in Asia and the Pacific islands also eat seaweed. Seaweed is one kind of algae.

The oceans give us oil and gas. Large deposits of oil have been found in the ground along the continental shelf. And usually, where there is oil, there is also natural gas.

The oceans give us minerals. Ocean water contains every known mineral. The most common one is, of course, common table salt. This is also called sodium chloride. It is taken from the ocean to be used in many ways. Other minerals that are taken from the sea are manganese and bromine. Still other minerals dissolved in the ocean are not used. It costs too much to take them out. But scientists are looking for ways to make mining the ocean floor less costly.

Phytoplankton are float-
ing plants. There are other
kinds of plankton. They
are microscopic animals
called <u>zooplankton</u> [zoh-
uh-PLANK-tun]. Both
types of plankton are the
start of the ocean food
chain. It works something
like this:

Figure A

- Tiny sea creatures eat the microscopic plankton.
- Small fish eat the tiny creatures.
- Larger fish eat the small fish.
- Still larger fish eat the large fish . . . and so on.

Actually, not only fish take part in this food chain. All sea animals are involved. They
include octopus, shellfish, and sea mammals like seals, dolphins, and whales.

How do people fit into this food chain? _____

SOMETHING INTERESTING

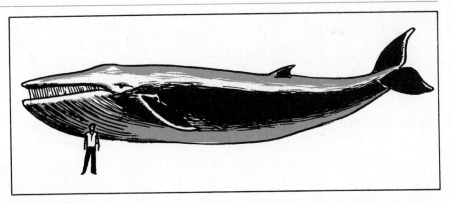

Figure B

Plankton are among the <u>smallest</u> life forms in the sea.

Whales are the <u>largest</u>. In fact, whales are the largest animals that ever lived.

The largest whale is the blue whale. It may grow 29 meters (95 feet) long and weigh 136
metric tons (150 tons).

The huge blue whale is a baleen whale. Baleen whales eat mostly plankton — about
1/2 to 1 1/2 tons every day.

So just think — the world's largest animals depend on some of the world's tiniest living
things.

Some fish do not taste good. People do not eat them. But they are still important. They have valuable nutrients—especially protein.

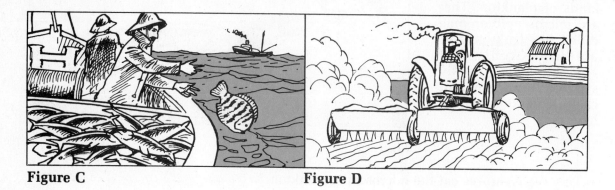

Figure C   **Figure D**

Some of these "trash" fish are made into fertilizer. How does this help farmers? _____

_____

_____

Figure E   *Desalination plant.*

Another important resource of the oceans is fresh water. In some countries, fresh water is very scarce. In these countries, people get their fresh water from removing the salt from the oceans.

In shallow offshore waters, drilling is done from permanent platforms. The platforms have legs that are sunk into the ocean floor.

In deeper water, floating platforms and special drilling ships are used.

Scientists believe that there is more oil below the oceans than there is below land.

What special problems does offshore drilling present? _____

_____

Figure F   *Drilling for offshore oil.*

FILL IN THE BLANK

Complete each statement using a term or terms from the list below. Write your answers in the spaces provided.

eat
salt
phytoplankton
shellfish
rain and snow

bromine
seaweed
dead
oil and natural gas
mineral

fertilizer
fish
manganese
ocean

1. Most of the oxygen we breathe comes from _____ .

2. Plankton live in the _____ .

3. The oceans supply most of the vapor that returns to earth as _____ .

4. Without the oceans, our planet would be a "_____ " planet.

5. People eat many things that live in the ocean. Three examples are _____ ,

   _____ , and _____ .

6. "Trash" fish are fish that are not good to _____ . They are made into

   _____ .

7. Large deposits of _____ have been discovered along coastal waters.

8. Ocean water contains every known _____ .

9. Three minerals we do take from sea water are _____ ,

   _____ , and _____ .

MATCHING

Match each term in Column A with its description in Column B. Write the correct letter in the space provided.

Column A	Column B
_____ 1. phytoplankton	a) some minerals we take from the sea
_____ 2. zooplankton	b) used for fertilizer
_____ 3. salt, manganese, bromine	c) supply most of the oxygen to the atmosphere
_____ 4. "trash" fish	d) change coastlines
_____ 5. waves	e) floating sea animals

TRUE OR FALSE

In the space provided, write "true" if the sentence is true. Write "false" if the sentence is false.

————— 1. Green plants give off oxygen.

————— 2. All green plants grow on land.

————— 3. Most of our oxygen comes from zooplankton.

————— 4. Most of our oxygen comes from phytoplankton.

————— 5. Phytoplankton are large.

————— 6. The ocean is an important source of food.

————— 7. Seaweed is a food.

————— 8. The oceans have only small deposits of oil.

————— 9. Every mineral we use comes from the ocean.

————— 10. Huge amounts of water evaporate from the ocean. This means that the oceans are drying out.

REACHING OUT

Many people earn their living from the sea.

How many different kinds of jobs can you name that depend upon the sea?—————

———————————————————————————————

———————————————————————————————

———————————————————————————————

The ocean is important for some of its harmful effects on people too. What are some ways

in which the oceans can harm people? —————————————————

———————————————————————————————

———————————————————————————————

———————————————————————————————

What is water pollution? | 7

LESSON 7 | What is water pollution?

You have learned about some of the "gifts" from the ocean. But, what have people given to the oceans in return? ... Oil spills, garbage, wastes from factories and ships — many kinds of harmful substances, or pollutants [puh-LOOT-ents].

Pollution is a major problem. Pollution is anything that harms the environment. Water pollution occurs when harmful substances enter the hydrosphere. Today, many lakes and rivers are polluted. They cannot be used for drinking or swimming. Some are so polluted that fish cannot live in them.

Now let us find out where water pollution comes from.

Sewage is a major source of water pollution. Germs live in sewage. Many fish and shellfish cannot be eaten because they contain germs that live in sewage.

Chemicals   Many chemicals pollute the water. Some chemicals are used on farmlands to help plants grow. Others are used to kill insect pests. These chemicals seep into the ground water. The ground water is carried to lakes and rivers.

Some harmful chemicals come from industry too. Some factories dump wastes directly into rivers. Other industries bury wastes in drums in the ground. But what happens if the drums rust and break apart? The wastes leak into the ground water. Where do they end up?

WHAT DO THE PICTURES SHOW?

The pictures below show different causes of water pollution. Match each cause with its picture. Choose from the following causes:

Sewage   Industrial wastes

Oil spill   Farm chemicals

Figure A

1. Cause? _____

Figure B

2. Cause? _____

Figure C

3. Cause? _____

Figure D

4. Cause? _____

Figure E

Some industries take cold water from a lake or stream. They use the water for cooling. Then they release the water back into its river or lake. Is the water the same? No! When the water is used for cooling, the water itself becomes heated. So when the water is put back into its source, it kills plants and animals that normally live in cooler water.

This kind of pollution is called thermal [THUR-mul] pollution. Nuclear power plants are the main cause of thermal pollution.

TRUE OR FALSE

In the space provided, write "true" if the sentence is true. Write "false" if the sentence is false.

————— 1. Pollution is not a major problem.

————— 2. Some factories dump wastes directly into rivers.

————— 3. Water pollution occurs when harmful substances enter the atmosphere.

————— 4. Thermal pollution occurs when water is cooled.

————— 5. Chemicals from farmland seep into ground water.

————— 6. Germs live in sewage.

————— 7. Pollutants of ground water are carried to lakes and rivers.

————— 8. Farms are the major cause of thermal pollution.

————— 9. Wastes buried in drums are not harmful to the environment.

————— 10. Oil spills are harmful to ocean wildlife.

Sewage-treatment plants have been built in many cities and towns. These plants change sewage into less harmful substances.

Figure F

Laws also help protect our water supply. Many farmland chemicals have been banned. They can no longer be used.

Laws require industries to clean their wastes before dumping them into lakes and rivers. Laws also call for the clean-up of wastes buried in drums in the ground.

Figure G

1. Why is water pollution a major problem? _____

   _____

2. a) How do laws help fight water pollution? _____

   _____

   b) What do you think should happen to people who break the law and illegally

   dump wastes into the water? _____

   _____

3. How can you help stop water pollution? _____

   _____

WORD SEARCH

The list on the left contains words that you have used in this Lesson. Find and circle each word where it appears in the box. The spellings may go in any direction: up, down, left, right, or diagonally.

pollution
water
sewage
germs
thermal
oil
fish
drums
harmful
wastes

P	A	J	R	L	G	S	H	P	S
W	O	K	L	E	J	H	M	L	E
A	I	L	R	P	I	S	N	U	W
S	L	M	L	O	C	I	A	F	A
T	S	G	B	U	O	F	Z	M	G
E	Y	F	X	R	T	B	E	R	E
S	N	I	E	F	D	I	R	A	D
M	U	T	Q	K	V	C	O	H	L
H	A	G	D	R	U	M	S	N	E
W	T	L	A	M	R	E	H	T	W

REACHING OUT

In the space below, draw a diagram that shows how a chemical used on a farm to kill insects, could end up in a person's body.

What is air made of?

8

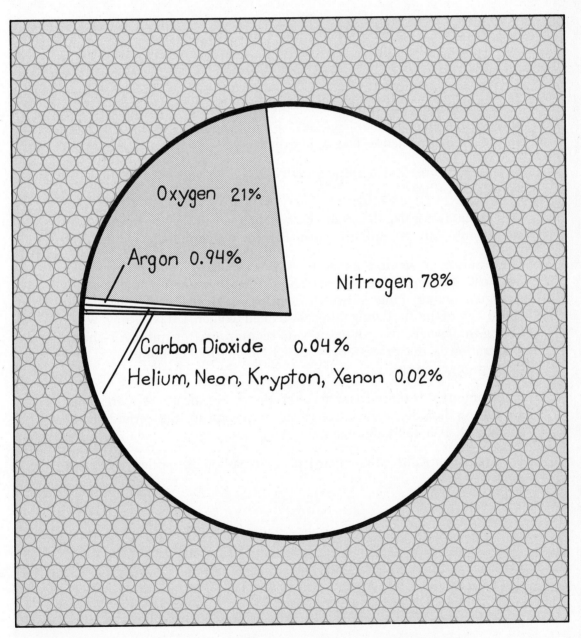

Oxygen 21%

Argon 0.94%

Nitrogen 78%

Carbon Dioxide 0.04%

Helium, Neon, Krypton, Xenon 0.02%

atmosphere [AT-mus-feer]: envelope of gases that surrounds the earth
respiration [res-puh-RAY-shun]: process by which living things combine food and
  oxygen to get energy

LESSON 8 | What is air made of?

Several Americans have walked on the moon. Some of them even rode among the craters in lunar "buggies." But the moon has no air of its own. So the astronauts had to take along their own—in tanks.

Take a deep breath. Go ahead—really do it! Do you need air tanks in order to breathe?

Our planet is not like the moon. Our planet has air. It is surrounded by an "ocean" of air. We call this ocean of air the **atmosphere** [AT-mus-feer].

The atmosphere, or air, is a mixture of gases. Nitrogen and oxygen make up most of this mixture. About 78% of the atmosphere is made up of nitrogen. Living things need nitrogen to survive. Oxygen makes up about 21% of the air. Living things also need oxygen. Do you know why? Living things need oxygen to carry on **respiration** [res-puh-RAY-shun]. Respiration is the process by which living things combine food and oxygen to get energy.

Small amounts of other gases make up the rest of the atmosphere. They are carbon dioxide, water vapor (water in gas form), and certain "rare" gases such as helium and neon.

The atmosphere also contains tiny pieces of solids like pollen, dust, and ash.

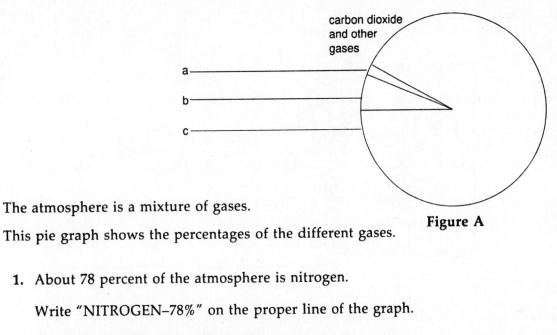

carbon dioxide
and other
gases

a

b

c

Figure A

The atmosphere is a mixture of gases.

This pie graph shows the percentages of the different gases.

1. About 78 percent of the atmosphere is nitrogen.

   Write "NITROGEN–78%" on the proper line of the graph.

2. About 21 percent of the atmosphere is oxygen.

   Write "OXYGEN-21%" on the proper line of the graph.

3. Figure this one out.

   If the atmosphere has 78 percent nitrogen and 21 percent oxygen . . .

   then

   what percent is left for carbon dioxide and the other gases? _____ percent

   Write this number on the proper line of the graph.

THE OXYGEN-CARBON DIOXIDE CYCLE

Oxygen and carbon dioxide constantly cycle through the environment. Animals breathe in oxygen for respiration. They gave off carbon dioxide as a waste product. Plants use the carbon dioxide to make their own food. Plants give off oxygen.

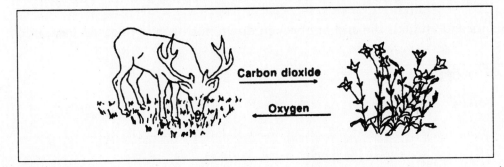

Carbon dioxide

Oxygen

Figure B

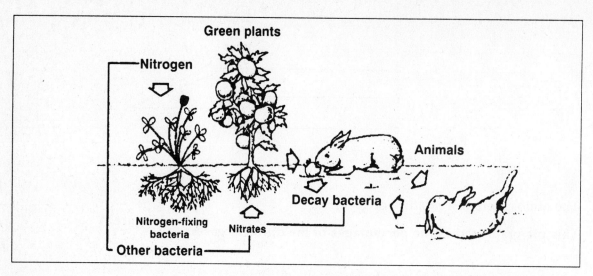

Figure C

Nitrogen makes up about 78% of the atmosphere. However, most living things cannot use nitrogen directly from the air. Bacteria (bak-TEER-ee-uh) are microscopic living things. Some bacteria in the soil change the nitrogen in the air into forms plants can use. Animals get the nitrogen they need by eating plants.

When plants and animals die, other kinds of bacteria break them down. The nitrogen is released back into the atmosphere.

Study Figures B and C to answer the following questions.

1. Animals take in _____ for respiration.

oxygen, carbon dioxide

2. Plants give off _____ when they make their own food.

oxygen, carbon dioxide

3. Nitrogen in the air is changed into forms most living things can use by

   _____ .

soil bacteria, plants

4. Animals get the nitrogen they need by eating _____ .

soil bacteria, plants

5. When plants and animals die and are broken down, nitrogen is released back into

   the _____ .

soil, atmosphere

Natural dust is formed in several ways:

Figure D *Dust comes from broken-up rocks.*

Figure E *Dust also comes from space.*

Rocks break into smaller pieces. Finally, they become the size of dust (Figure D).

Some dust comes from meteors that burn up in the atmosphere. Much more dust comes from deep outer space (Figure E).

Space dust adds about two million metric tons a year to the earth's weight. That's about 4 1/2 billion pounds!

And here's a surprise. Some household dust is made up of flaked off skin cells!

FILL IN THE BLANK

Complete each statement using a term or terms from the list below. Write your answers in the spaces provided.

78%	nitrogen	rare
21%	atmosphere	mixture of gases
water vapor		

1. The "ocean" of air that surrounds the earth is called the _____ .

2. The atmosphere is made up of a _____ .

3. Water in gas form is called _____ .

4. Most of the atmosphere is made up of the gas _____ .

5. Nitrogen makes up about _____ of the atmosphere.

6. Oxygen makes up about _____ of the atmosphere.

7. Helium and neon are _____ gases.

MATCHING

Match each term in Column A with its description in Column B. Write the correct letter in the space provided.

Column A

_____ 1. atmosphere

_____ 2. water vapor

_____ 3. oxygen

_____ 4. dust, pollen, and smoke particles

_____ 5. respiration

Column B

a) needed by all living things

b) tiny solids in the atmosphere

c) mixture of gases that surrounds the earth

d) energy-producing process

e) water in the gas form

TRUE OR FALSE

In the space provided, write "true" if the sentence is true. Write "false" if the sentence is false.

_____ 1. Carbon dioxide is a "rare" gas.

_____ 2. The moon has no air of its own.

_____ 3. Soil bacteria change nitrogen gas into forms plants can use.

_____ 4. The atmosphere is a mixture of gases.

_____ 5. Most of the atmosphere is oxygen.

_____ 6. Oxygen makes up about 21 percent of the atmosphere.

_____ 7. Only animals need oxygen.

_____ 8. Water vapor is a gas.

_____ 9. Some dust is a natural part of the atmosphere.

_____ 10. Animals take in oxygen for respiration.

What are some properties of air?

9

properties [PROP-ur-tees]:   characteristics used to describe an object

LESSON 9 | What are some properties of air?

What is this book made of—metal or paper? It is made of paper, of course. But how do you know? You know from its **properties** [PROP-ur-tees].

Properties are characteristics used to describe an object. They help us describe matter. Properties also help us to tell one kind of matter from another.

There are many kinds of properties. Some common properties are state, weight, hardness, color, shape, and odor.

Air has certain properties. Let us examine three properties of air.

AIR IS INVISIBLE

The natural gases of the air have no color. You cannot see them.

AIR HAS MASS

Air is matter. It is made up of atoms and molecules. Atoms and molecules have mass. This means that air has mass.

AIR TAKES UP SPACE

Air also takes up space. Think about blowing up a balloon. When you blow air into a balloon, the balloon gets larger. It gets larger as air takes up space.

So far, you have learned that:

$$\text{AIR} \begin{cases} \text{is invisible.} \\ \text{has mass.} \\ \text{takes up space.} \end{cases}$$

You will learn more about these properties on the following pages.

SEEING IS BELIEVING

Look at Figure A. Then answer the questions.

1. What is inside the glass?

   _____

2. What property of air is shown here?

   _____

   _____

Figure A

PROVING THAT AIR HAS MASS

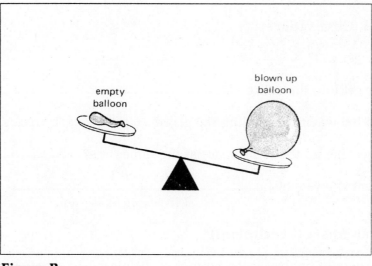

empty
balloon

blown up
balloon

Figure B

Without air in them, both balloons in Figure B have the same mass.

1. Which balloon has more mass, A or B? _____

2. Balloon _____ has more mass because it has _____ in it.

3. What property of air does this show? _____

   _____

51

What You Need (Materials)

drinking glass   piece of paper
large bowl (or sink)   water

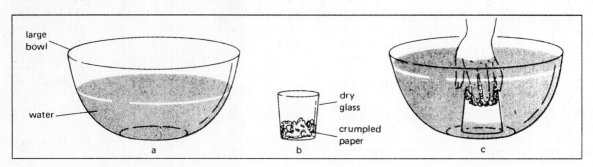

How To Do the Experiment (Procedure)

1. Fill a large bowl (or your sink) halfway with water (Figure a).

2. Stuff a piece of paper into a small glass. Push it all the way to the bottom (Figure b).

3. Turn the glass upside down. Hold it straight. Put it into the bowl (Figure c). Hold it there for a short time. Then lift the glass out.

4. Look at the paper in the glass. Then take the paper out and feel it.

What You Learned (Observations)

1. Did the paper get wet? _____

2. Did the water get into the entire glass? _____

3. What stopped the water from filling the glass? _____

4. Can two things take up the same space at the same time? _____

5. This experiment shows that _____ .

                           air has mass, air takes up space

Something to Think About (Conclusions)

What do you think would happen if the bottom of the glass had a hole in it? _____

_____

_____

How would you explain that? _____

_____

_____

Complete each statement using a term or terms from the list below. Write your answers in the spaces provided.

molecules	space	air has mass
nitrogen	water vapor	see
properties	gases	air is invisible
air takes up space	invisible	mass

1. Air is a mixture of ——————— .

2. We cannot——————— the gases of the air.

3. The word that means "not capable of being seen" is ——————— .

4. Air is made up of atoms and ——————— .

5. Atoms and molecules have ——————— and take up ——————— .

6. Characteristics that help us identify matter are called ——————— .

7. This lesson discussed three properties of air. They are: ——————— ,

   ——————— , ——————— .

8. The gas that makes up most of the air is——————— .

9. Water in gas form is called——————— .

TRUE OR FALSE

In the space provided, write "true" if the sentence is true. Write "false" if the sentence is false.

———— 1. You can see the gases of the air.

———— 2. Dust is invisible.

———— 3. Most of the time we do not see dust because dust is very small.

———— 4. Air is made up of molecules.

———— 5. Atoms and molecules have no mass.

———— 6. Atoms and molecules take up space.

———— 7. Air has mass.

———— 8. Air takes up space.

———— 9. Air has mass and takes up space because it is invisible.

WORD SCRAMBLE

Below are several scrambled words you have used in this Lesson. Unscramble the words and write your answers in the spaces provided.

1. SMAS   _____

2. IRA   _____

3. PPSETREORI   _____

4. EIINBSLIV   _____

5. SEPCA   _____

REACHING OUT

Figure D

A balloon filled with helium gas floats away.

1. Does this mean that helium does not

   have mass? _____

2. What does it mean? _____

   _____

   _____

What is air pollution?

10

What is air pollution?

Look at Figure A on the facing page. What do you see coming out of the cars, buses, and chimneys? Many air pollutants are being released into the air. Air pollution occurs when these harmful substances enter the atmosphere.

The burning of fossil fuels is the major cause of air pollution. Cars and factories use fossil fuels to run.

There are two kinds of air pollutants — solid particles and gases. Dust and soot are tiny particles. They are air pollutants. Dust and soot are given off in smoke. They can remain in the air for a long time. Dust and soot can irritate your eyes, and your lungs.

Many cities have a smog problem. Smog is a mixture of smoke, fog, and gas pollutants, such as carbon monoxide. Smog is harmful to people who have breathing problems.

Gas pollutants can also harm the environment indirectly. For example, sulfur dioxide is a pollutant gas. It combines with water in the atmosphere to form acids. The acids fall to the earth as acid rain. Acid rain damages statues and buildings. It also kills living things in lakes and streams. It kills trees too.

Figure A

Look at Figure A. It shows some of the ways air becomes polluted. Identify each source by writing its name next to the correct letter on the spaces provided.

a) _____   e) _____

b) _____   f) _____

c) _____   g) _____

d) _____   h) _____

Answer the following.

1. What is the major cause of air pollution? _____

   _____

2. What are the three fossil fuels? _____

   _____

3. What are fossil fuels used for? _____

   _____

What You Need (Materials)

hand lens   toothpick
microscope slide   petroleum jelly

How To Do the Experiment (Procedure)

1. Use the toothpick to coat one side of a glass slide with a thin layer of petroleum jelly.

2. Place the slide on a window ledge overnight.

3. Examine the slide with a hand lens the next day.

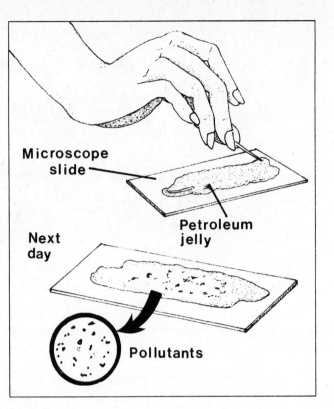

Figure B

What You Learned (Observations)

1. What are some of the things you saw on your slide? _____

_____

Something To Think About (Conclusions)

1. What do you think these particles are? _____

2. Where do you think they come from? _____

Complete each statement using a term or terms from the list below. Write your answers in the spaces provided. Some words may be used more than once.

soot   acid rain   break
fossil fuels   atmosphere   gas
cities   chemicals   eyes
lungs

1. The major cause of air pollution is the burning of _____.

2. Air pollution occurs when harmful substances are released into the

    _____ .

3. Two kinds of pollutants in smoke are dust and _____ .

4. Smog is a mixture of smoke, fog, and _____ .

5. Some gases that are released into the atmosphere combine with water in the air to

    form _____ .

6. Dust and soot can irritate your _____ and _____ .

7. Many _____ have a smog problem.

8. Acid rain can cause brick, stone, and metal structures to _____ apart.

9. Sulfur dioxide is a pollutant _____ .

10. Cars use _____ to run.

Complete the chart by identifying the pollutant or pollutants that are contained in each item described in the first column. Place a check mark in the correct column or columns.

	Source	Smoke	Dust	Soot	Chemicals
1.	Burning fossil fuels				
2.	Smog				
3.	Factory smokestacks				
4.	Automobile exhaust				
5.	Burning wood in a fireplace				

TRUE OR FALSE

In the space provided, write "true" if the sentence is true. Write "false" if the sentence is false.

_____ 1. Dust and soot are gas pollutants.

_____ 2. Smog is harmless.

_____ 3. Acid rain kills forests and fish.

_____ 4. Smog is made up of smoke, fog, and chemicals.

_____ 5. Smog is a major problem in small towns.

_____ 6. The burning of fossil fuels is the major cause of air pollution.

_____ 7. Carbon monoxide is a pollutant gas.

_____ 8. Carpooling does not reduce air pollution.

_____ 9. Dust and soot may remain in the air for a long time.

_____ 10. Gas pollutants can harm the environment indirectly.

WORD SCRAMBLE

Below are several scrambled words you have used in this Lesson. Unscramble the words and write your answers in the spaces provided.

1. SGOM   _____

2. TNPOULLTSA   _____

3. IRA   _____

4. BNGNRUI   _____

5. OTOS   _____

What are the layers of the atmosphere?

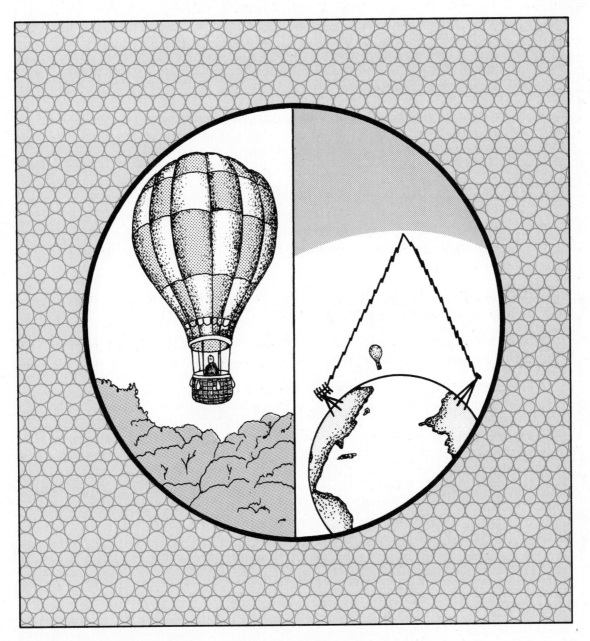

ionosphere [Y-on-uh-sferr]: upper layer of the atmosphere
stratosphere [STRAT-uh-sfeer]: middle layer of the atmosphere
troposphere [TROHP-uh-sfeer]: lowest layer of the atmosphere

LESSON 11 | What are the layers of the atmosphere?

Wood floats on water because wood is lighter than water. A rock sinks because it is heavier than water. A balloon filled with helium floats away because helium is lighter than air.

The atmosphere is made up of gases of different weights. Some gases are lighter than others. Gases in the atmosphere arrange themselves according to weight. The heavier gases are closest to the earth's surface. The lighter ones are higher up.

The atmosphere begins at the earth's surface and goes more than 50 km into space. Not all parts of the atmosphere are the same. Scientists have divided the atmosphere into three main layers. They are the **troposphere** [TROHP-uh-sfeer], the **stratosphere** [STRAT-uh-sfeer] and the **ionosphere** [Y-on-uh-sfeer].

TROPOSPHERE   The troposphere is the lowest layer of the atmosphere. We live in the troposphere. It is the heaviest layer.

Weather occurs in the troposphere. Winds occur in this layer. The higher you go in the troposphere, the colder it gets.

STRATOSPHERE   The stratosphere is above the troposphere. There is no weather in the stratosphere.

A layer of <u>ozone</u> [OH-zohn] is found in the stratosphere. Ozone is a form of oxygen. It stops most of the harmful rays of the sun from reaching the earth.

IONOSPHERE   The ionosphere is above the stratosphere. It is made up of particles called ions.

Radio waves bounce off the ionosphere. Conditions in the ionosphere allow us to send radio messages around the world.

Figure A shows the layers of the atmosphere. Study the diagram and then answer the questions.

1. Name the three layers of the atmosphere. Start with the lowest layer and name them

   in order _____ , _____ , _____ .

2. Is the troposphere the same height everywhere? _____

3. What is the height range of the troposphere? _____

4. In which layer do airplanes fly? _____

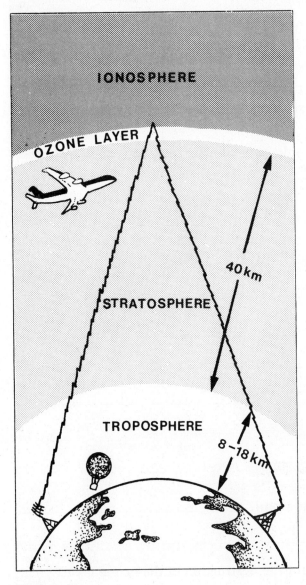

Figure A

5. In which layer is the ozone layer

   found? _____

6. About how many km is the

   stratosphere? _____

Which layer . . .

7. has the most air? _____

   _____

8. has the least air? _____

   _____

9. In which layer does most weather

   take place? _____

   _____

10. In which layer are radio waves

    reflected? _____

    _____

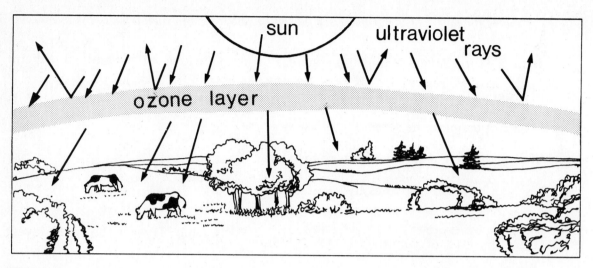

Figure B

In addition to the light that we can see, the sun gives off <u>ultraviolet rays</u>. Ultraviolet rays are invisible — but if you have ever had a sunburn you have felt their effect. Ultraviolet rays cause sunburn.

Living things need ultraviolet rays — but only in small amounts. Too much ultraviolet light is dangerous. It can cause skin cancer.

That is where the ozone layer comes in. The ozone layer filters out ultraviolet light. It is our natural "sunscreen."

In 1985, scientists discovered a hole in the ozone layer. The hole is getting bigger. Scientists think that the ozone layer is being destroyed by pollution.

1. In which layer is ozone found? _____

2. What is ozone? _____

3. Why is ozone important? _____

   _____

4. a) Do living things need ultraviolet light? _____

   b) How much? _____
      small amounts, large amounts

5. a) Why is too much ultraviolet light harmful? _____

   _____

   b) Why must we all be concerned about the destruction of the ozone layer?

   _____

TRUE OR FALSE

In the space provided, write "true" if the sentence is true. Write "false" if the sentence is false.

_____   1. The atmosphere is made up of four main layers.

_____   2. The place where the troposphere ends is called the ionosphere.

_____   3. Ozone is a form of oxygen.

_____   4. The higher you go in the troposphere the colder it gets.

_____   5. Ozone stops most of the ultraviolet light from the sun.

_____   6. The stratosphere is the closest layer to the earth's surface.

_____   7. The ionosphere is the middle layer of the atmosphere.

_____   8. Radio waves bounce off the ionosphere.

_____   9. All the gases in the atmosphere weigh the same.

_____ 10. Weather occurs in the troposphere.

COMPLETE THE CHART

Decide which layer of the atmosphere is described by each characteristic listed in the table. Place a check mark in the proper column.

	Characteristic	Ionosphere	Stratosphere	Troposphere
1.	Contains a layer of ozone			
2.	Weather takes place here			
3.	Made up of ions			
4.	Airplanes travel here			
5.	Most winds occur here			
6.	Allows radio signals to be sent across the earth			

In the space below, draw a diagram that shows the layers of the atmosphere. Include these labels on your diagram: **troposphere, stratosphere, ozone layer,** and **ionosphere.** Draw **clouds** and an airplane in the layer in which they would most likely be located.

REACHING OUT

Why do you think airplanes travel in the stratosphere? (What is the benefit?)

_____

_____

How does the sun heat the atmosphere?

conduction [kon-DUCK-shun]:   movement of heat through a solid
convection [kon-VEK-shun]:   movement of heat through a liquid or a gas
radiation [ray-dee-AY-shun]:   movement of energy through empty space

LESSON 12 | How does the sun heat the atmosphere?

Without the sun, there would be no life on earth. Plants need the sun to help them grow. Without plants we would have no food to eat and no oxygen to breathe. The sun also gives us warmth. The sun heats the atmosphere and all the lands and waters.

When the sun's light is absorbed by the earth's surface, it is changed to heat. Heat does not stay in one place. It moves from place to place. Heat moves in three ways—**conduction** [kon-DUCK-shun], **convection** [kon-VEK-shun], and **radiation** [ray-dee-AY-shun].

CONDUCTION   Heat moves through solids by conduction. In conduction, vibrating molecules pass on heat from molecule to molecule.

CONVECTION   Heat moves through gases and liquids by convection. In convection, heated molecules move away from the heat. Cooler molecules take their place. Then they become heated, too.

When air is heated, it expands. As warm air expands, it becomes lighter. Warm air is lighter than cool air. Warm air rises. Cooler, heavier air sinks.

RADIATION   Conduction and convection need molecules to work. Radiation does not. Radiation is the movement of light or heat energy through empty space.

Now let us trace the sun's energy.

- The sun is about 150 million kilometers from Earth. Most of this distance is empty space where there are almost no atoms or molecules. Such an empty space is called a vacuum. Energy from the sun moves through this vacuum by radiation.

- The sun's energy then hits the atmosphere. The air molecules become heated by convection.

- The sun's energy reaches the land and water on earth. The water becomes heated by convection. The land becomes heated by conduction. Air that touches the warm surface also becomes heated by conduction.

Some of the heat from the land and water reflects back into the atmosphere. This warms the atmosphere even more.

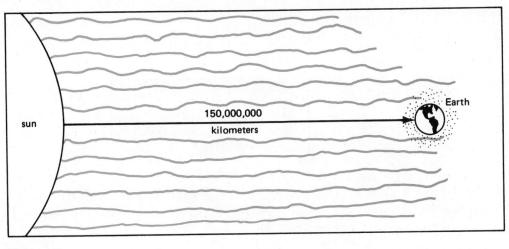

Figure A

1. Most of the distance between the sun and the earth is _____ .
   <u>air, empty space</u>

2. The sun's energy moves through outer space by _____ .
   <u>conduction, convection, radiation</u>

3. Radiation _____ need atoms and molecules to work.
   <u>does, does not</u>

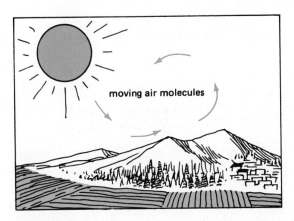

Figure B

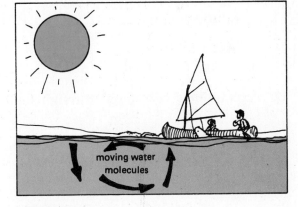

Figure C

4. Heat moves through gases and liquids by _____ .
   <u>conduction, convection, radiation</u>

5. Convection _____ need atoms and molecules to work.
   <u>does, does not</u>

6. What are liquids and gases made of? _____

69

7. After atoms and molecules of gases and liquids are heated, they _____ .
    rise, sink

8. Warm air is _____ than cool air.
    lighter, heavier

Figure D

9. Heat moves through solids by _____ .
    conduction, convection, radiation

10. Conduction _____ need atoms and molecules to work.
    does, does not

11. What are solids made of? _____

12. Explain how heat moves through solids. _____

    _____

13. How is some of the atmosphere heated by conduction? _____

    _____

FILL IN THE BLANK

Complete each statement using a term or terms from the list below. Write your answers in the spaces provided. Some words may be used more than once.

expands
atmosphere
radiation
convection

atoms and molecules
conduction
rises

1. The three ways that heat moves from place to place are _____,

_____ , and _____ .

2. Heat moves through solids by _____ .

3. Heat moves through liquids and gases by _____ .

4. Heat moves through empty space by _____ .

5. In conduction and convection, heat is carried by _____ .

6. When air is heated, it _____ .

7. As warm air expands, it _____ .

8. Heat moves through the atmosphere by _____ .

9. Rocks and soil are heated by _____ .

10. Some of the heat from the land and water bounce back into the

_____ .

MATCHING

Match each term in Column A with its description in Column B. Write the correct letter in the space provided.

Column A	Column B
_____ 1. sun	a) the way heat moves through empty space
_____ 2. conduction	b) mixture of gases
_____ 3. convection	c) warms our entire planet
_____ 4. radiation	d) the way heat moves through gases and liquids
_____ 5. atmosphere	e) the way heat moves through solids

TRUE OR FALSE

In the space provided, write "true" if the sentence is true. Write "false" if the sentence is false.

_____ **1.** Heat stays in one place.

_____ **2.** Heat moves only where there are atoms and molecules.

_____ **3.** Heat moves in three different ways.

_____ **4.** In solids, heat moves by convection.

_____ **5.** In gases and liquids, heat moves by convection.

_____ **6.** Conduction and convection need atoms and molecules.

_____ **7.** In empty space heat moves by radiation.

_____ **8.** There are many atoms and molecules in outer space.

_____ **9.** The earth gets its heat from the sun.

_____ **10.** Heat can be reflected.

REACHING OUT

In what simple way can you show that the earth bounces some heat back into the atmosphere? (You need no instruments to do this—only your hand.)

_____

_____

_____

_____

_____

_____

_____

What is air pressure?

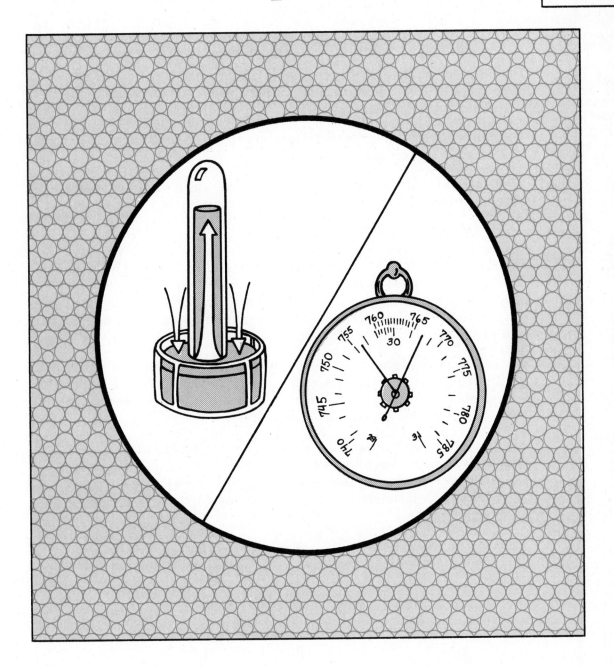

13

LESSON 13 | What is air pressure?

What keeps you from floating into space?

There is a force called gravity that pulls things towards the earth. This force keeps you from floating away Gravity also keeps the gases of the air from escaping into space.

The pull of gravity is stronger the closer you are to the earth's center. The pull becomes weaker the farther you go from the earth's center.

Most molecules of the air are held close to the earth's surface where gravity is strong. There are fewer and fewer molecules the higher up you go.

The atmosphere reaches up almost 1000 kilometers (600 miles). You have already learned that air has weight. Weight is a force. The weight of the air above the earth's surface pushes down on the surface. This force is called **air pressure**. At sea level a column of air on one square inch weighs about 1 kilogram. Air pressure is 1 kilogram per 1 square centimeter.

The pull of gravity results in more gas molecules at sea level than higher up. Therefore, the air pressure is greater closer to the ground. The higher you go above sea level, the lesser the air pressure. The lower you go below sea level, the greater the air pressure.

Air presses on every surface, even your body. On every square inch of your body, there is 15 pounds of air pressure. This could add up to more than 10 tons of air pressing against you. Why then, does the air not crush you? The answer is simple: Air does not press downward. <u>Air presses in all directions.</u>

There is air inside your body too. This air presses <u>outward</u> with the same force as the air that is pressing inward. This keeps you from being crushed.

Figure A *Air does not press like this.*   *Air presses like this.*

Look at Figure A.

1. Air presses _____ .

only downward, only upward, in all directions

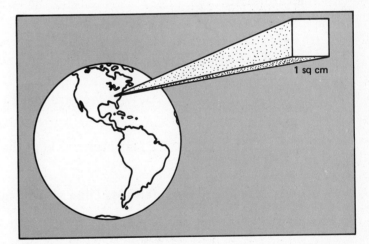

Figure B

At sea level, a column of air resting on one square centimeter (1 sq cm) weighs 1 kilogram (kg).

2. What gives air its weight? _____

3. The air pressure at sea level is _____ kilogram per square _____ .

What You Need (Materials)

glass tumbler
water
thin cardboard

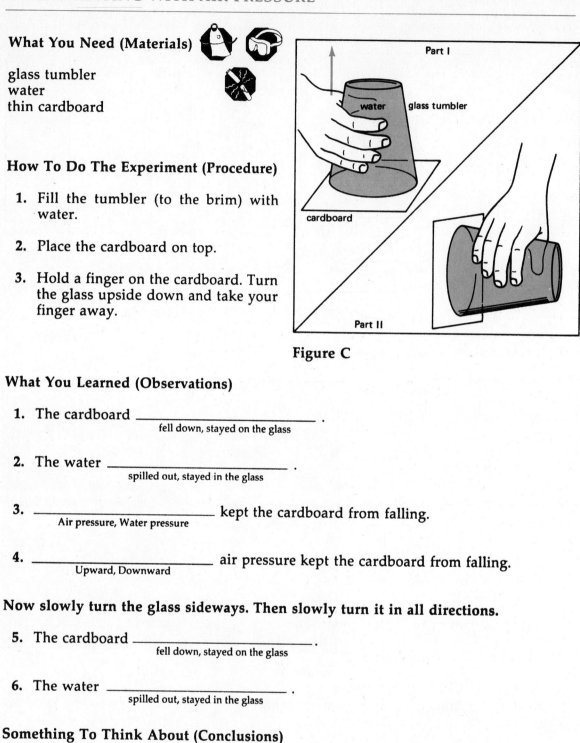

Figure C

How To Do The Experiment (Procedure)

1. Fill the tumbler (to the brim) with water.

2. Place the cardboard on top.

3. Hold a finger on the cardboard. Turn the glass upside down and take your finger away.

What You Learned (Observations)

1. The cardboard _____ .
   fell down, stayed on the glass

2. The water _____ .
   spilled out, stayed in the glass

3. _____ kept the cardboard from falling.
   Air pressure, Water pressure

4. _____ air pressure kept the cardboard from falling.
   Upward, Downward

Now slowly turn the glass sideways. Then slowly turn it in all directions.

5. The cardboard _____ .
   fell down, stayed on the glass

6. The water _____ .
   spilled out, stayed in the glass

Something To Think About (Conclusions)

1. _____ kept the cardboard from falling down.
   Air pressure, Water pressure

2. We have shown that air presses _____ .
   only up, only down, only to the sides, in every direction

76

Figure D

Answer each of the following questions with *Sea Level City*, *Valleyville*, or *Mountaintop*.

1. Air pressure is greatest at _____ .

2. Air pressure is weakest at _____ .

3. Air pressure is 1 kg per sq cm at _____ .

4. Air pressure is greater than 1 kg per sq cm at _____ .

5. Air pressure is less than 1 kg per sq cm at _____ .

FILL IN THE BLANK

Complete each statement using a term or terms from the list below. Write your answers in the spaces provided.

earth's surface	gravity	weaker	less
1000 kilometers	1 kg per sq cm	valley	mountain
directions			

1. The force that pulls objects toward the earth's surface is called _____ .

2. Gravity is strongest close to the _____ .

3. As you go higher, gravity becomes _____ .

4. Air presses in all _____ .

5. The higher you go, the _____ air there is.

6. The atmosphere reaches up about _____ in space.

7. At sea level, air presses with a force of about _____ .

8. Air pressure is usually greater in a _____ than it is on a

_____ .

SCIENCE *EXTRA*

Reducing Pollution

Take a deep breath. Better yet, do not! Pollution . . . Let's face it . . . We cannot eliminate it, but we can reduce it. Pollution's effects are spread out over many years. In fact, until pollution's harmful effects are felt, most of us do not seem to be affected by it.

Fortunately, there are other people who have dedicated themselves to alerting the nation and the world of the dangers of pollution. These environmental groups are in part, responsible for the Clean Air Act of 1970.

The Clean Air Act of 1970 was revised in 1977, and then again in October of 1990. The revision made the Act much stronger and carried stiffer fines for offenders. In addition to pollution-control devices on cars, and the reduction of CFC production, the revised law includes some new points. These new points included:

- Strict limits on industrial pollutants that cause acid rain;
- The elimination of chemicals that break down the ozone layer;

- A reduction in the amount of poisonous and cancer-causing chemicals; and
- The reduction of dangerous auto emission.

To protect industry, and jobs, the new Clean Air rules will be phased in slowly—over 15 years.

The government also has set up the Environmental Protection Agency (EPA). The EPA was established to protect the nation's environment from pollution. The EPA has provided funds to clean up hazardous waste sites as well as prosecute violators. However, one agency cannot solve the problem of pollution itself.

Even individuals can do something to save the environment. Recycle your glass, aluminum, plastic and paper. Use public transportation, walk, or ride a bicycle instead of driving. Buy products in spray pumps rather than in spray cans. If every person was aware of the danger of pollution and did something about it, the problem of pollution could be reduced.

What makes air pressure change?

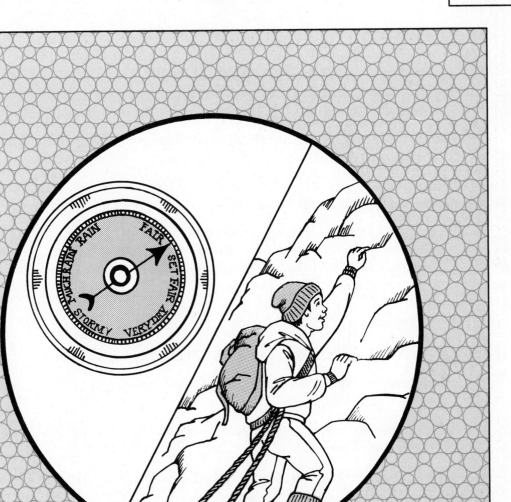

barometer [buh-ROM-uh-ter]:   instrument used to measure air pressure

LESSON 14 | What makes air pressure change?

Where is air pressure greater, Mount Everest or Death Valley? Death Valley is <u>below</u> sea level. It has a greater air pressure.

However, air pressure changes even without going from mountains to valleys.

Two other things can change air pressure. They are <u>temperature</u> and the <u>amount of water vapor in the air.</u>

TEMPERATURE   Heat makes air molecules move faster. As they move faster, the molecules spread farther apart. A container of warm air has <u>fewer</u> molecules in it than an equal container of cool air.

Fewer molecules mean less weight. And less weight means less pressure.

WARM AIR WEIGHS LESS THAN COOL AIR.

WARM AIR HAS LESS PRESSURE THAN COOL AIR.

AMOUNT OF WATER VAPOR   Water vapor weighs less than most of the other gases of the air.

Each molecule of water vapor that goes into the air takes the place of some of the air molecules.

Usually, a heavier molecule is replaced. This makes the air lighter.

MOIST AIR WEIGHS LESS THAN DRY AIR.

MOIST AIR HAS LESS PRESSURE THAN DRY AIR.

LET US REVIEW

Review what you learned about air pressure in Lesson 13. Then look at Figure A and answer the questions. Write the correct letter in the spaces provided.

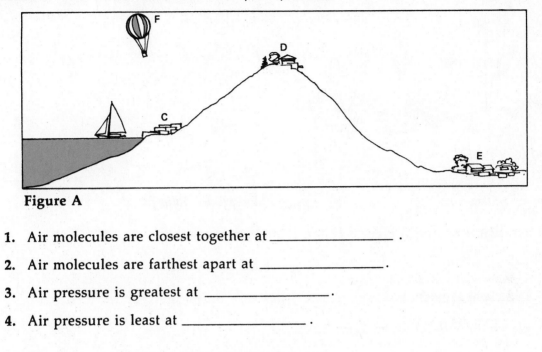

Figure A

1. Air molecules are closest together at _____ .

2. Air molecules are farthest apart at _____ .

3. Air pressure is greatest at _____ .

4. Air pressure is least at _____ .

TEMPERATURE CHANGES AIR PRESSURE

Study Figures B and C. Then answer the questions by writing B or C on the spaces provided.

Figure B

Figure C

1. Which beaker has the warmer air? _____

2. Which beaker has the cooler air? _____

3. Which beaker has more air molecules? _____

4. Which beaker has fewer air molecules? _____

5. Air is lighter in beaker _____ .

6. Air is heavier in beaker _____ .

7. Air pressure is greater in beaker _____ .

8. Air pressure is less in beaker _____ .

Figure D *Desert*

Figure E *Rain forest*

The two places shown in Figures D and E are both at sea level.

1. The air in Figure _____ has a lot of water vapor.

2. The air in Figure _____ has very little water vapor.

3. Which air is heavier?_____

4. Which air is lighter? _____

5. Air pressure is greater in _____ .

6. Air pressure is weaker in _____ .

ABOUT BAROMETERS

Air pressure can be measured with a **barometer** [buh-ROM-uh-ter]. One kind of barometer is a mercury barometer. It is made of a glass tube filled with mercury.

How does it work?

- The tube is open at one end.
- The open end is placed in a container of mercury.
- Air pressure pushes down on the surface of the mercury in the container.
- The mercury is pushed up the tube.
- At sea level, air pressure can support, or hold up, a column of mercury 760 mm (about 30 inches) high.
- When air pressure increases, the mercury in the tube rises a little.
- When air pressure decreases, the mercury in the tube falls.

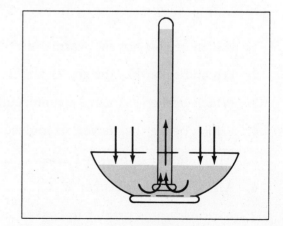

Figure F

Another barometer is the aneroid [AN-uh-royd] barometer. This is the barometer that is commonly used to measure air pressure.

Figure G

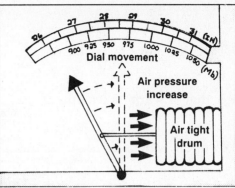

Figure H

The aneroid barometer has a small drum with almost no air in it. A needle is connected to the drum. The drum is "squeezed" when air pressure increases. This moves the needle to a greater number.

FILL IN THE BLANK

Complete each statement using a term or terms from the list below. Write your answers in the spaces provided. Some words may be used more than once.

molecules	height above sea level	presses
less	atoms	weight
temperature	barometer	pressure
gases	amount of water vapor in the air	higher

1. The atmosphere is a mixture of _____ .

2. Gases are made up of _____ and _____ .

3. Atoms and molecules have _____ .

4. Anything that has weight also _____ against things.

5. Three things that can change air pressure are: _____ ,

   _____ and _____ .

6. Air pressure becomes weaker the _____ up you go.

7. Warm air has less _____ than cool air.

8. Moist air weighs _____ than dry air.

9. Air with a lot of water vapor has less _____ than dry air.

10. An instrument that measures air pressure is called a _____ .

COMPLETING SENTENCES

Choose the correct word or term for each statement. Write your choice in the spaces provided.

1. Molecules move faster in _____ air.
   _{warm, cool}

2. Air that is warm takes up _____ space than cool air.
   _{more, less}

3. Warm air weighs _____ than cool air.
   _{more, less}

4. Warm air has _____ pressure than cool air.
   _{more, less}

5. Water vapor is a _____ .
   _{liquid, gas}

6. Water vapor molecules weigh _____ than most of the other gases in the air.
   _{more, less}

7. Moist air is _____ than dry air.
   _{heavier, lighter}

8. Moist air has _____ pressure than dry air.
   _{more, less}

9. The higher you go, the _____ air there is.
   _{more, less}

10. Air pressure is _____ on a mountain than at sea level.
    _{greater, less}

REACHING OUT

1. Why do mountain climbers have trouble breathing on high mountains?

   _____

   _____

2. Mountain A and Mountain B are the same height. At their tops the temperatures are the same. But Mountain B is covered by very moist air. Which mountain has the greater air pressure? Why?

   _____

   _____

   _____

84

What is a wind?

15

anemometer [an-uh-MOM-uh-tur]: instrument used to measure wind speed
wind: horizontal movement of air
wind vane: instrument used to measure wind direction

LESSON 15 | What is a wind?

You cannot see wind. But you know it is there. You can feel it pressing against your body. You see tree branches bend when it blows. A gentle wind makes you feel fresh. A strong wind can blow you down.

What is this invisible force we call wind?

A **wind** is air that is moving parallel to the ground. (Air that moves up or down is not called wind.)

There are two main groups of winds. They are global winds and local winds.

GLOBAL WINDS move across our entire planet. They cover very large areas.

Most of the time a global wind blows at the same speed and in the same direction. Some global winds blow high in the atmosphere. You cannot always feel them on the ground.

LOCAL WINDS move across small areas. They change direction and speed very often. Local winds blow low in the atmosphere. You can always feel them on the ground.

Every wind has speed and direction. How can you measure wind? There are two instruments that are used, an **anemometer** [an-uh-MOM-uh-tur], and a **wind vane.** An anemometer measures how fast a wind blows. A wind vane tells us from which direction a wind blows.

Do you want to know what causes winds? You will find out in the next Lesson.

Winds have names. The name of a wind tells us where the wind comes from. For example, sea breezes and land breezes are two kinds of local winds. A <u>sea breeze</u> comes from the sea. It moves toward the land. A <u>land breeze</u> comes from the land and moves toward the sea.

Winds are also named by compass direction. In fact, most winds are named this way. For example, in North America, the important global winds come from the west. They are called the prevailing westerlies.

A compass has four main direction points. They are: north (N), east (E), south (S), and west (W) (Figure A).

The directions between these main points are: northeast (NE), southeast (SE), southwest (SW), and northwest (NW).

A north wind comes from the north. It moves towards the south.

A southwest wind blows from the southwest. It heads towards the northeast.

COMPASS DIRECTIONS

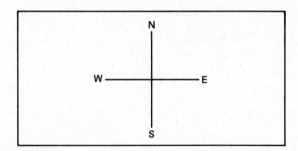

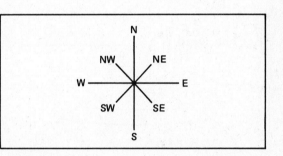

Figure A *The four main points of a compass.*

Figure B *The four in-between compass points.*

1. N stands for _____ .

2. S stands for _____ .

3. E stands for _____ .

4. W stands for _____ .

5. Opposite of north is _____ .

6. Opposite of south is _____ .

7. Opposite of east is _____ .

8. Opposite of west is _____ .

9. NE stands for _____ .

10. SE stands for _____ .

11. SW stands for _____ .

12. NW stands for _____ .

13. Opposite of northeast is _____ .

14. Opposite of southeast is _____ .

15. Opposite of southwest is _____ .

16. Opposite of northwest is _____ .

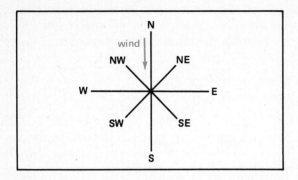

Figure C

1. The wind shown here is coming

   from the _____ .

2. It is heading towards the

   _____ .

3. The wind is a _____
   wind.

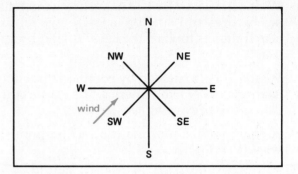

Figure D

4. The wind shown here is coming

   from the _____ .

5. It is moving towards the

   _____ .

6. The wind is a _____
   wind.

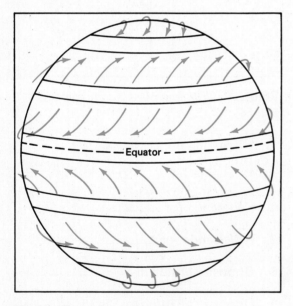

Figure E

Look at Figure E. The arrows show the
directions of the main global winds.

7. Do they all blow in the same

   direction? _____

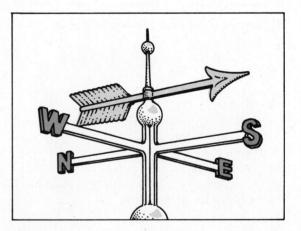

Figure F

Figure F shows a wind vane.

8. Where is the wind coming from?

   _____

9. This wind is a _____
   wind.

WIND SPEED

Figure G shows an anemometer.

1. What does an anemometer measure?

   _____

A wind makes the anemometer's cups turn.

2. The stronger the wind, the

   _____ the cups turn.
      slower, faster

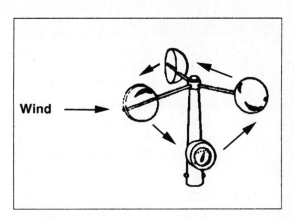

Wind →

Figure G

FILL IN THE BLANK

Complete each statement using a term or terms from the list below. Write your answers in the spaces provided. Some words may be used more than once.

anemometer	air	direction
global	high	always
speed	wind vane	local
parallel to the ground	ground	

1. A wind is _____ that is moving _____ .

2. The two main groups of winds are _____ winds and

   _____ winds.

3. Winds that move across the entire planet are called _____ winds.

4. Some planetary winds blow _____ in the atmosphere.

5. You cannot feel some global winds on the _____ .

6. A global wind usually blows at the same _____ and

   _____ .

7. Winds that move across small parts of the earth are called _____
   winds.

8. Local winds can _____ be felt on the ground.

9. Local winds often change _____ and _____ .

10. An _____ measures wind speed; a _____ shows wind
    direction.

COMPLETE THE CHART

Complete the chart by filling in the missing information. Put a check in the proper box.

		Global Wind	Local Wind
1.	Covers small area		
2.	Often changes speed and direction		
3.	Covers large area		
4.	Always felt on the ground		
5.	Can be high above the ground		
6.	Speed and direction stays the same		

TRUE OR FALSE

In the space provided, write "true" if the sentence is true. Write "false" if the sentence is false.

_____   1. You need air to have a wind.

_____   2. The moon has winds.

_____   3. Air that moves up or down is a wind.

_____   4. There is only one kind of wind.

_____   5. Global winds cover large areas.

_____   6. All global winds blow high in the atmosphere.

_____   7. Global winds often change speed and direction.

_____   8. Local winds cover small areas.

_____   9. You can always feel a local wind.

_____ 10. Local winds often change speed and direction.

The arrows on this map stand for winds. Study each arrow. Then fill in the chart below the map.

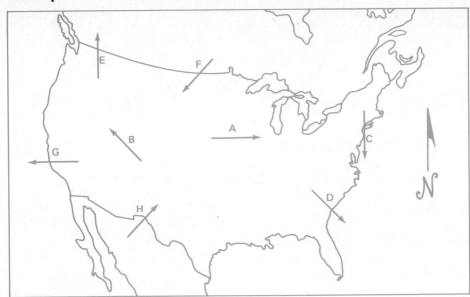

Figure H

Wind	Coming From Which Direction?	Heading Towards Which Direction?	Wind Name
A			
B			
C			
D			
E			
F			
G			
H			

MATCHING

Match each term in Column A with its description in Column B. Write the correct letter in the space provided.

Column A

_____ **1.** compass

_____ **2.** wind vane

_____ **3.** N, S, E, W

_____ **4.** SW wind

_____ **5.** NE wind

Column B

a) main compass points

b) heads NE

c) turns with the wind

d) comes from the NE

e) tells direction

FILL IN THE BLANK

Complete each statement using a term or terms from the list below. Write your answers in the spaces provided. Some words may be used more than once.

north   northeast   east
southwest   west   wind
wind vane   northwest   south
compass direction   comes from   southeast

1. Air moving parallel to the ground is called _____ .

2. A _____ tells us from which direction a wind blows.

3. Most winds are named by _____ .

4. A wind's name is the direction the wind _____ .

5. The main points of the compass are _____ , _____ ,

    _____ , and _____ .

6. Four in-between compass points are _____ , _____ ,

    _____ , and _____ .

7. Opposite of northwest is _____ .

8. Opposite of west is _____ .

9. A southwest wind come from the _____ .

10. A south wind blows toward the _____ .

REACHING OUT

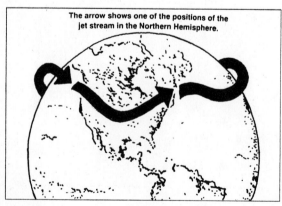

The arrow shows one of the positions of the jet stream in the Northern Hemisphere.

Figure I

In the 1940s, global winds were discovered by B-17 pilots during World War II. These global winds are called jet streams. They are high-speed winds in the upper atmosphere. Their speeds may be as high as 500 km/hour. The jet streams flow from west to east. Why do you think airplanes traveling in the jet stream gain speed going from west to east, but lose speed going from east to west?

_____

_____

_____

What causes wind?

air currents [KUR-unts]:   up and down movements of air

LESSON 16 | What causes wind?

In Lesson 4, you learned about <u>ocean currents</u>. Now you will learn about **air currents** [KUR-unts]. Air currents are up-and-down movements of air. They are important in making winds.

You have learned that the sun heats our entire planet. However, the sun does not heat all parts of the earth the same. Some areas of the earth are heated more than others. This causes air currents.

Warm air and cool air do not weigh the same. Warm air is lighter than cool air. And you know that light air rises.

When warm air rises, other cooler air rushes in to take its place. The air that rushes in moves parallel to the ground. It is this moving air that we call "wind."

Wind is caused by the uneven heating of the earth's surface.

• Uneven heating of the entire planet causes global winds.
• Uneven heating of smaller areas causes local winds.

You will learn more about how winds are made on the next page.

Study Figure A carefully. Then choose the correct term to complete each statement. Write your choice in the space.

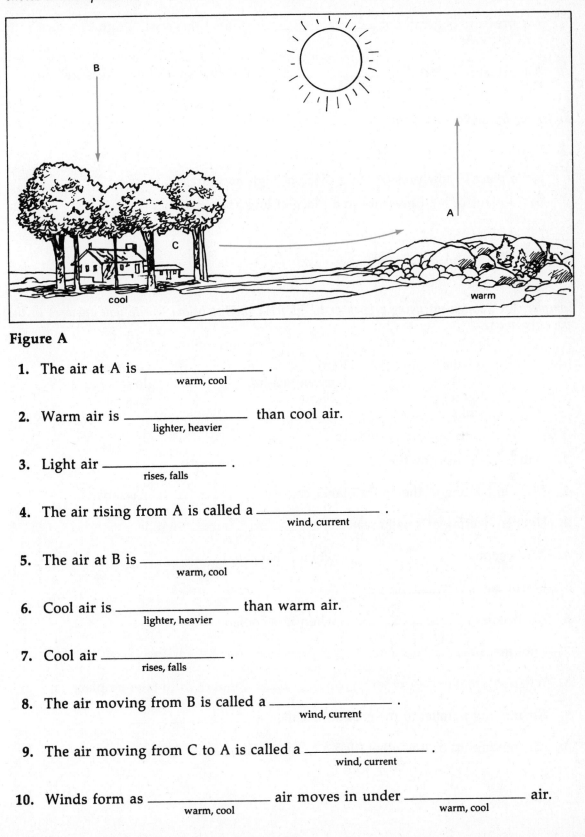

cool

warm

Figure A

1. The air at A is ––––––––––––––––––– .
   warm, cool

2. Warm air is ––––––––––––––––––– than cool air.
   lighter, heavier

3. Light air ––––––––––––––––– .
   rises, falls

4. The air rising from A is called a ––––––––––––––––––– .
   wind, current

5. The air at B is ––––––––––––––––––– .
   warm, cool

6. Cool air is ––––––––––––––––––– than warm air.
   lighter, heavier

7. Cool air ––––––––––––––––– .
   rises, falls

8. The air moving from B is called a ––––––––––––––––––– .
   wind, current

9. The air moving from C to A is called a ––––––––––––––––––– .
   wind, current

10. Winds form as ––––––––––––––––– air moves in under ––––––––––––––––– air.
    warm, cool   warm, cool

Now that you know how winds form, try to answer these questions. Refer to Lesson 14 if you have to.

1. Air pressure is greater at _____ . Label this spot "High Pressure" on Figure A.

A, C

2. Air pressure is less at _____ . Label this spot "Low Pressure" on Figure A.

A, C

Underline the correct statement.

3. Wind moves from

   a) a place of low pressure to a place of high pressure

   b) a place of high pressure to a place of low pressure

FILL IN THE BLANK

Complete each statement using a term or terms from the list below. Write you answers in the spaces provided.

heavier	local	cooler air
wind	uneven heating	global
lighter	current	rises
sinks		

1. Winds are causes by the _____ of the earth.

2. Uneven heating of the entire planet causes _____ winds.

3. Uneven heating of small areas cause _____ winds.

4. Air becomes _____ when it is heated.

5. Warm air _____ .

6. Air becomes _____ when it is cooled.

7. Cool air _____ .

8. When warm air rises, other _____ moves in to take its place.

9. Air moving parallel to the ground is called a _____ .

10. Air moving up or down is called a _____ .

MATCHING

Match each term in Column A with its description in Column B. Write the correct letter in the space provided.

Column A	Column B
_____ 1. wind	a) moves up or down
_____ 2. current	b) falls
_____ 3. heated air	c) moves over small areas
_____ 4. cooled air	d) moves parallel to the ground
_____ 5. local winds	e) rises

TRUE OR FALSE

In the space provided, write "true" if the sentence is true. Write "false" if the sentence is false.

_____ 1. Warm air weighs less than cool air.

_____ 2. Warm air has greater pressure than cool air.

_____ 3. Cool air is heavier than warm air.

_____ 4. Cool air has greater pressure than warm air.

_____ 5. Warm air rises.

_____ 6. Cool air rises.

_____ 7. Wind moves from a cool place to a warm place.

_____ 8. Rising or falling air is called a wind.

_____ 9. A wind moves parallel to the ground.

_____ 10. All winds move at the same speed.

WORD SCRAMBLE

Below are several scrambled words you have used in this Lesson. Unscramble the words and write your answers in the spaces provided.

1. GLBAOL _____

2. DIWN _____

3. RERNUCT _____

4. COLLA _____

5. NEEVUN _____

MULTIPLE CHOICE

In the space provided, write the letter of the word that best completes each statement.

———————— **1.** Wind is caused by

    a) ocean currents.   **b)** uneven cooling.

    c) land breezes.   **d)** uneven heating.

———————— **2.** The earth is heated by

    a) currents.   **b)** wind.

    c) the sun.   **d)** the moon.

———————— **3.** As air is cooled

    a) it rises.   **b)** it becomes lighter.

    c) it sinks.   **d)** its pressure decreases.

———————— **4.** Up-and-down movements of air are called

    a) currents.   **b)** breezes.

    c) winds.   **d)** convections.

———————— **5.** Warm air

    a) falls.   **b)** rises.

    c) sinks.   **d)** remains in place.

REACHING OUT

Wind moves from high pressure to low pressure. What makes some winds stronger than others?

————————————————

————————————————

————————————————

————————————————

————————————————

Figure B

What are shore breezes? 17

land breeze: breeze coming from the land toward the sea
sea breeze: breeze coming from the sea towards the land

LESSON 17 | What are shore breezes?

Did you ever visit the seashore? Did you notice that it is usually breezy there?

Shore breezes are special, gentle local winds. There are two kinds of shore breezes-the **sea breeze** and the **land breeze.**

A sea breeze moves in from the sea. It heads towards the land. A sea breeze blows during the daytime.

A land breeze moves out from the land. It heads towards the sea. A land breeze blows during the evening hours.

Shore breezes are caused by the uneven heating and cooling of the land and water.

SEA BREEZE During the daytime, the sun heats both the land and the water, but the land heats up faster than the water. Because of this, the air above the land becomes warmer than the air above the water.

The cooler and heavier air that is over the water moves in toward the land. The warmer and lighter air above the land is pushed upward.

This air that moves in from the sea and heads towards the land is a sea breeze.

LAND BREEZE In the evening, the sun goes down. The land and water cool off, but the land cools off faster than the water. The water becomes warmer than the land.

The warmer and lighter air above the water rises. Cooler and heavier air that is over the land moves in to take its place.

This air that moves out from the land and heads towards the sea is a land breeze.

Study Figure A and Figure B on the next page. Then choose the correct term to complete the statements below each picture. Write your choice in the space provided.

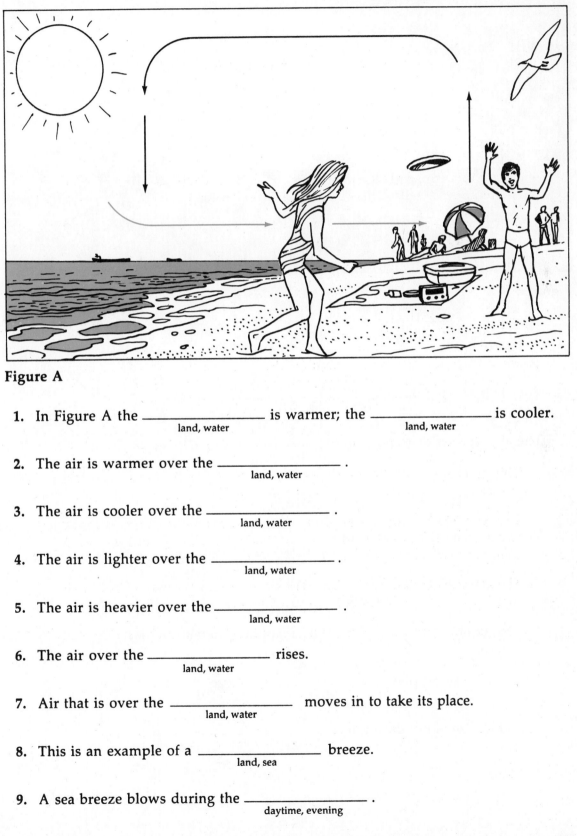

Figure A

1. In Figure A the _____ is warmer; the _____ is cooler.

land, water   land, water

2. The air is warmer over the _____ .

land, water

3. The air is cooler over the _____ .

land, water

4. The air is lighter over the _____ .

land, water

5. The air is heavier over the _____ .

land, water

6. The air over the _____ rises.

land, water

7. Air that is over the _____ moves in to take its place.

land, water

8. This is an example of a _____ breeze.

land, sea

9. A sea breeze blows during the _____ .

daytime, evening

Figure B

1. In Figure B, the _____ is warmer; the _____ is cooler.
   _{land, water}   _{land, water}

2. The air is warmer over the _____ .
   _{land, water}

3. The air is cooler over the _____ .
   _{land, water}

4. The air is lighter over the _____ .
   _{land, water}

5. The air is heavier over the _____ .
   _{land, water}

6. The air over the _____ rises.
   _{land, water}

7. Air that is over the _____ moves in to take its place.
   _{land, water}

8. This is an example of a _____ breeze.
   _{land, sea}

9. A land breeze blows during the _____ .
   _{daytime, evening}

FILL IN THE BLANK

Complete each statement using a term or terms from the list below. Write your answers in the spaces provided. Some words may be used more than once.

land   breeze   land breeze
more slowly   sea   faster
sea breeze   daytime   evening

1. Any gentle wind is called a _____ .

2. The two kinds of shore breezes are the _____ and the

   _____ .

3. A sea breeze blows during the _____ .

4. A sea breeze blows from the _____ and moves toward the

   _____ .

5. A land breeze blows during the _____ .

6. A land breeze blows from the _____ and moves towards the

   _____ .

7. Land heats up _____ than water.

8. Land cools off _____ than water.

9. Water heats up _____ than land.

10. Water cools off _____ than land.

MATCHING

Match each term in Column A with its description in Column B. Write the correct letter in the space provided.

Column A	Column B
_____ 1. land breeze	a) heats up fast and cools fast
_____ 2. sea breeze	b) heats up slowly and cools slowly
_____ 3. water	c) starts from the land and moves toward the sea
_____ 4. land	d) rises
_____ 5. warm air	e) starts from the sea and moves towards the land

Look at Figures C and D. Then complete the exercise that goes with each picture.

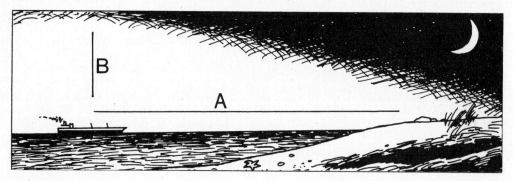

Figure C

Lines A and B stand for moving air.

1. Draw arrows on each line to show how it is moving.

2. The current is line _____ .
   <small>A, B</small>

3. The shore breeze is line _____ .
   <small>A, B</small>

4. What kind of shore breeze is it? _____

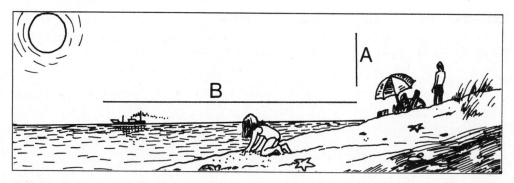

Figure D

Lines A and B stand for moving air.

5. Draw arrows on each line to show how it is moving.

6. The current is line _____ .
   <small>A, B</small>

7. The shore breeze is line _____ .
   <small>A, B</small>

8. What kind of shore breeze is it? _____

A monsoon is like a very strong shore breeze. It covers a very large area. It is caused by the uneven heating and cooling of land and water areas. But a monsoon does not change from day to night. A monsoon changes from season to season.

Monsoons happen in India and southeast Asia.

The maps below show the monsoon winds of India.

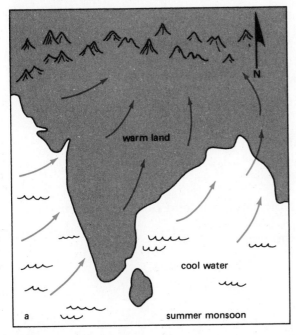

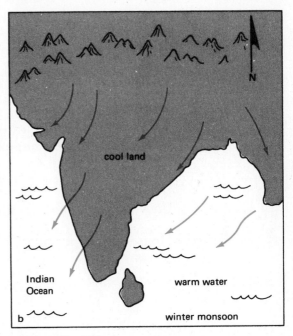

Figure E *Summer monsoon*

Figure F *Winter monsoon*

During the summer, the continent remains warm both day and night. Monsoon winds blow from the sea to the land all summer.

This wind has a lot of moisture from the water. It causes heavy rain.

During the winter, the land gets cold. The air above the oceans is warmer. Monsoon winds blow from the land to the water all winter.

The wind is dry. There is little rain in winter.

1. In the summer, monsoon winds blow _____ the land.
   <u>towards, away from</u>

2. In the winter, monsoons blow _____ the land.
   <u>towards, away from</u>

3. In the summer, monsoon winds are _____ .
   <u>wet, dry</u>

4. In the winter, monsoon winds are _____ .
   <u>wet, dry</u>

5. The monsoon winds change with _____ .
   <u>each day, the seasons</u>

TRUE OR FALSE

In the space provided, write "true" if the sentence is true. Write "false" if the sentence is false.

—————— **1.** Sea breezes and land breezes are global winds.

—————— **2.** A sea breeze is a daytime breeze.

—————— **3.** A land breeze is an evening breeze.

—————— **4.** A land breeze comes from the sea.

—————— **5.** Land heats up faster than water.

—————— **6.** Land cools off faster than water.

—————— **7.** A monsoon is like a huge shore breeze.

—————— **8.** A monsoon covers a small area.

—————— **9.** Uneven heating and cooling of water and land cause monsoons.

—————— **10.** Monsoons happen all over the world.

REACHING OUT

Sometimes it gets cool extra fast at night. Would this make a land breeze blow slower or faster? Why? ——————————————————————

——————————————————————————————

——————————————————————————————

——————————————————————————————

——————————————————————————————

What are valley and mountain breezes?

18

mountain breeze: cool air that moves down from a mountain
valley breeze: cool air that moves up from a valley

LESSON 18 | What are valley and mountain breezes?

Do you live near a mountain? People who live near mountains often feel special, gentle local winds. They are called **valley breezes** and **mountain breezes.**

Valley breezes and mountain breezes are caused by the uneven heating and cooling of mountains and valleys.

VALLEY BREEZE During the day, the air on a mountaintop is warmer than the air in valleys. The cooler air in the valleys moves up the mountaintop.

The air that moves up from the valley is called a valley breeze.

MOUNTAIN BREEZE At night, air begins to cool down. The side of the mountain cools off very fast. So does the air close to it. The valley is sheltered so it keeps some of its heat. The cooler and heavier air from the mountain begins to flow down the slope. It moves into the valley below.

This air that moves down from the mountain is called a mountain breeze.

Look at Figures A and B. Then complete the sentences about each picture.

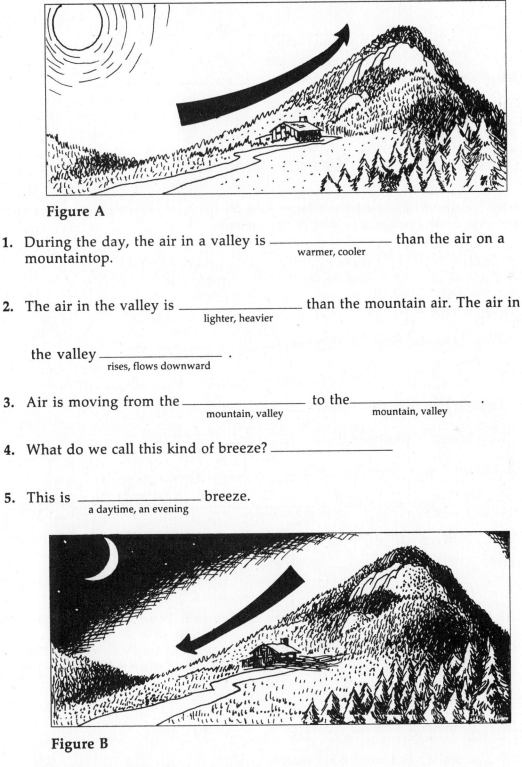

Figure A

1. During the day, the air in a valley is _____ than the air on a
    mountaintop.
    <small>warmer, cooler</small>

2. The air in the valley is _____ than the mountain air. The air in
    <small>lighter, heavier</small>

    the valley _____ .
    <small>rises, flows downward</small>

3. Air is moving from the _____ to the _____ .
    <small>mountain, valley</small>   <small>mountain, valley</small>

4. What do we call this kind of breeze? _____

5. This is _____ breeze.
    <small>a daytime, an evening</small>

Figure B

6. When the sun goes down, the air _____
    cools more rapidly.
    <small>in the valley, on the mountaintop</small>

7. This cooler air is _____ than warm air. The mountain
   _{heavier, lighter}

   air _____ .
   _{rises, flows downward}

8. Air is moving from the _____ to the _____ .
   _{mountain, valley}   _{mountain, valley}

9. What do we call this kind of breeze? _____ .

10. This is _____ breeze.
    _{a daytime, an evening}

FILL IN THE BLANK

Complete each statement using a term or terms from the list below. Write your answers in the spaces provided. Some words may be used more than once.

cooler	warmer	valley
daytime	evening	mountain

1. A valley breeze blows during the _____ .

2. A mountain breeze blows during the _____ .

3. A valley breeze blows from a _____ .

4. A mountain breeze blows from a _____ .

5. A valley breeze blows toward a _____ .

6. A mountain breeze blows toward a _____ .

7. During the day, air in a valley is _____ than air on a mountaintop.

8. During the day, air on a mountaintop is _____ than air in a valley.

MATCHING

Match each term in Column A with its description in Column B. Write the correct letter in the space provided.

Column A	Column B
_____ 1. valley breeze occurs	a) local winds
_____ 2. mountain breeze occurs	b) sinks
_____ 3. valley and mountain breezes	c) at night
_____ 4. warm air	d) rises
_____ 5. cool air	e) during the day

TRUE OR FALSE

In the space provided, write "true" if the sentence is true. Write "false" if the sentence is false.

_____ 1. Valley breezes and mountain breezes are local winds.

_____ 2. Valley breezes and mountain breezes are caused by the uneven heating and cooling of the land and water.

_____ 3. A valley breeze blows during the daytime.

_____ 4. A valley breeze blows from a mountain.

_____ 5. A mountain breeze blows during the daytime.

NAME THE BREEZE

One of these figures below shows a valley breeze. The other one shows a mountain breeze. Write **Figure C** *or* **Figure D** *on the spaces provided.*

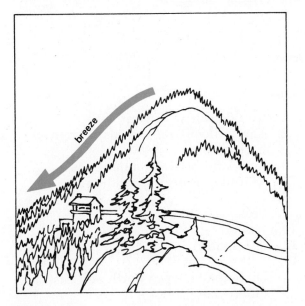

Figure C

Figure D

1. Which figure shows the valley breeze? _____

2. Which one is the mountain breeze? _____

3. Which one happens at night? _____

4. Which one happens during the daytime? _____

Use the clues to complete the crossword puzzle.

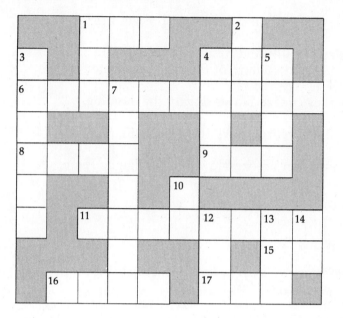

Clues

Across

1. Large body of water
4. What you wear on your head
6. Measures wind speed
8. Tilt
9. Black and sticky substance
11. Land above a valley
15. Direction opposite SW
16. Shows wind direction
17. A writing tool

Down

1. You do this with your eyes
2. Larger than a mouse (also 9 across/ backwards)
3. Low land between mountains
4. Warming energy from the sun
5. Rip
7. Seasonal wind
10. Not off
12. Hit lightly
13. Old time hotel
14. Direction between north and east (abbreviate)

REACHING OUT

On nights when it is cloudy, the air close to the mountainside does not cool as rapidly.

Would this make the mountain breeze flow faster or slower? Explain. _____

_____

_____

_____

What is weather?

weather: day to day conditions of the atmosphere

LESSON 19 | What is weather?

We probably talk about weather more often than anything else. How often have you started talking to people by saying, "Wow, look at that rain!" or "This heat is too much!"? Weather affects us in many ways. We dress according to the weather. We make plans hoping for fair weather.

Weather is very, very important to everyone. But, what exactly is **weather.**

Weather is the day-to-day conditions of the atmosphere. It is different from place to place, and weather is always changing.

Several things make up weather. They are:

• air temperature

• air pressure

• appearance of the sky (clear or cloudy)

• wind speed

• wind direction

• humidity (amount of water in the air)

• precipitation [prih-sip-uh-TAY-shun] (rain, snow, sleet, hail)

You will learn more about weather in the next Lessons. You also will learn how to read a weather map. In fact, you will learn to make your own weather map. It's easy-and it's fun.

Weather affects the lives and jobs of many people. For example, it affects how, or even if, we get from place to place.

Figure A

Figure B

Figure C

Figure D

Figure E

Figure F

Weather also affects how we play.

Figure G

Figure H

1. Can you think of other ways in which we are affected by the weather? _____

    _____

2. Name a kind of job that is affected by the weather. _____

    _____

WHAT DO THE PICTURES SHOW?

Look at each picture. Each of the pictures below hints at some part of weather. On the line under each picture, write the part of weather you think it shows. Choose from the list below.

humidity   appearance of sky   precipitation
air pressure   wind speed and direction temperature

Figure I

1.

Figure J

2.

Figure K

3. _____

Figure L

4. _____

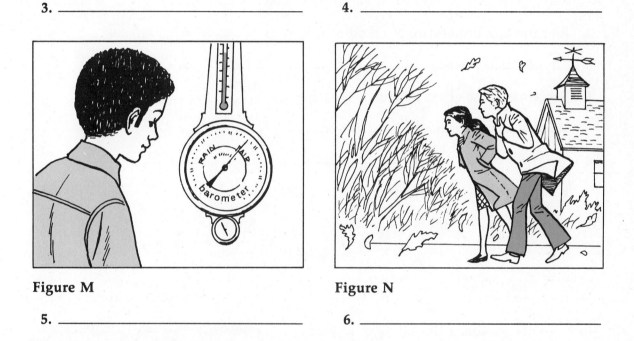

Figure M

5. _____

Figure N

6. _____

TRUE OR FALSE

In the space provided, write "true" if the sentence is true. Write "false" if the sentence is false.

_____ **1.** Air pressure is part of the weather.

_____ **2.** Weather takes place in the troposphere. (Look back to Lesson 11 if you have to.)

_____ **3.** Weather is the same everywhere.

_____ **4.** Weather can change quickly.

_____ **5.** Water is always a liquid.

FILL IN THE BLANK

Complete each statement using a term or terms from the list below. Write your answers in the spaces provided. Some words may be used more than once.

hot   how something looks   water
weighs   wind direction   clouds
wind speed   gas   precipitation
cold

1. Air pressure has to do with how much the air ——————— .

2. Temperature tells us how ——————— or ——————— the air is.

3. Rain, snow, hail, sleet, and drizzle are examples of ——————— .

4. Precipitation is made up of liquid or frozen ——————— .

5. "Appearance" means ——————— .

6. The appearance of the sky can be changed by ——————— .

7. "20 kilometers per hour" can describe ——————— .

8. "Northwest" can describe ——————— .

9. Humidity is the amount of ——————— in the air.

10. Water vapor is water in the ——————— form.

REACHING OUT

How can the weather affect the price of food?

_____

_____

_____

Figure O

What is relative humidity?

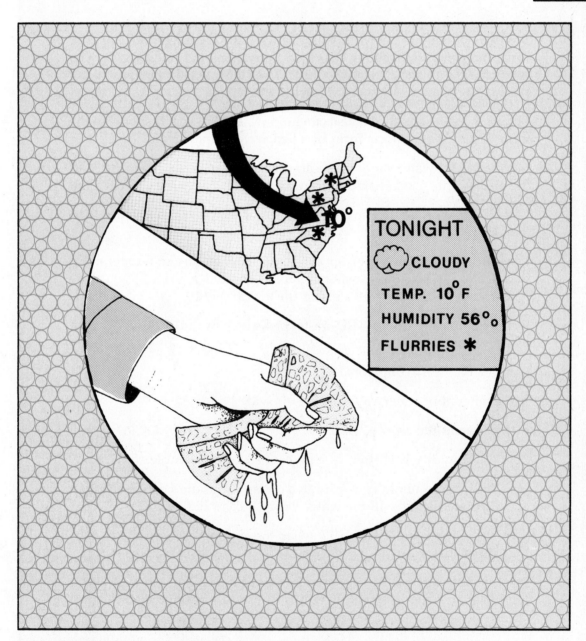

relative humidity [hyoo-MID-uh-tee]:   amount of water vapor in the air
    compared to the amount of water vapor the air can hold
water vapor: water in the gas form found in air

LESSON 20 | What is relative humidity?

Try this: Fill a large pan with water. Then place a sponge into the pan. What happens? The sponge soaks up the water—but not all of it. The sponge soaks up water until it is "full." Then it cannot soak up any more. We say the sponge is saturated [sach-uh-RAYT-ed].

The air is like a sponge. Air also can hold water. Water in the air is in the form of gas. Water in gas form is called **water vapor.**

The amount of water vapor in the air does not stay the same. Sometimes the air has only a small amount of water vapor. Sometimes it has a lot.

The air only can hold so much water vapor. When there is more than that, there is precipitation.

The amount of water vapor air can hold depends on the temperature. Warm air can hold more water vapor than cold air. The higher the temperature, the more water vapor the air can hold.

Relative humidity [hyoo-MID-uh-tee] tells us how "full" the air is with water vapor.

Relative humidity compares

• the amount of water vapor in the air with

• the amount the air can hold.

Relative humidity is written as a percent (%). For example:

(a) The relative humidity of saturated air is one hundred percent (100%). Saturated air has all the water vapor it can hold.

(b) The relative humidity is 50% when the air holds only half the water vapor that it can.

Relative humidity can be very low. It can reach near zero percent. But it can never be at zero percent. Even the driest air has some water vapor.

STUDYING RELATIVE HUMIDITY

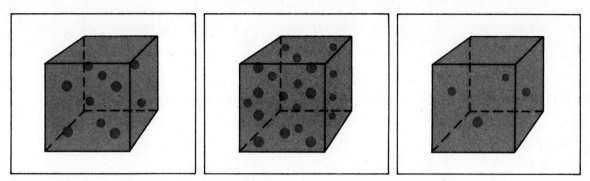

Figure A   **Figure B**   **Figure C**

Each cube stands for a part of the air. The temperature of each is 24° C (75° F). The balls stand for water vapor. You know that there are other gases in the air. Only water vapor is shown.

Write the letter of the correct cube in the blank.

1. Which air has the least water vapor? _____

2. Which air has the most water vapor? _____

3. Which air is the driest? _____

4. Which air is the dampest? _____

5. Which air has the highest relative humidity? _____

6. Which air has the lowest relative humidity? _____

7. What do you think? Which air may have rain soon? _____

MATCHING

Match each term in Column A with its description in Column B. Write the correct letter in the space provided.

	Column A		Column B
_____	1. water vapor	a)	can hold less water vapor
_____	2. percent	b)	gas
_____	3. saturated	c)	filled up
_____	4. cold air	d)	can hold more water vapor
_____	5. warm air	e)	part of one hundred

Complete each statement using a term or terms from the list below. Write your answers in the spaces provided. Some words may be used more than once.

saturated	water vapor	damp
less	little	relative humidity
100%	more	lot

1. Water in the gas form is called _____ .

2. Dry air has a _____ water vapor.

3. Moist air has a _____ of water vapor.

4. Cold air can hold _____ water vapor than warm air.

5. The higher the temperature, the _____ water vapor air can hold.

6. The lower the temperature, the _____ water vapor air can hold.

7. Air that holds all the water vapor it can is called _____ air.

8. Saturated air feels very _____ .

9. The amount of water vapor in the air compared to the amount it can hold is called

   _____ .

10. The highest relative humidity is _____ .

UNDERSTANDING PERCENTAGES

One hundred percent (100%) is a full amount of anything. For example:	Fifty percent (50%) is one-half of anything. For example:
• 100 parts of 100 is 100% • 50 parts of 50 is 100% • 2 parts of 2 is also 100%	• 50 parts of 100 is 50% • 25 parts of 50 is 50% • 1 part of 2 is 50%

Now see if you can figure out these percents.

1. 100% of 20 is _____ .
   100, 20, 120

3. 25% of 20 is _____ .
   5, 25, 45

2. 50% of 20 is _____ .
   20, 70, 10

4. 10% of 20 is _____ .
   2, 20, 10

Each cube in Figures D-H stands for a part of the air. The temperatures are the same. Each ball stands for one part of water vapor.

In this example, you can assume that twenty parts of water vapor make each cube saturated. Twenty parts of water vapor is all that the air can hold at this temperature. With twenty parts of water vapor, the air has 100% relative humidity.

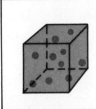 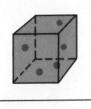 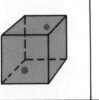 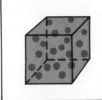 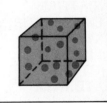

Figure D   **Figure E**   **Figure F**   **Figure G**   **Figure H**

Study each diagram. Then answer these questions. (Use Figure letters.)

1. **a)**   Which cube of air is saturated? _____

    b)   What is the relative humidity of the air in this cube? _____

    c)   Can this air hold any more water vapor? _____

2. Which air has

    a)   50% relative humidity? _____   **c)**   25% relative humidity? _____

    b)   75% relative humidity? _____   **d)**   10% relative humidity? _____

3. Which air is the driest? _____

4. Which air is the dampest? _____

5. Which air can hold these many more parts of water vapor?

    a)   18 _____   **c)**   10 _____

    b)   5 _____   **d)**   15 _____

DO YOU REMEMBER?

Air has many other gases. When more and more water vapor is added, it makes the other gases spread out more.

This makes the air pressure _____ . If you do not remember, look back
<u>stronger, weaker</u>
to Lesson 11.

WORD SEARCH

The list on the left contains words that you have used in this Lesson. Find and circle each word where it appears in the box. The spellings may go in any direction: up, down, left, right, or diagonally.

PRECIPITATION
HUMIDITY
WEATHER
TEMPERATURE
SKY
RELATIVE
HOT
SATURATE
VAPOR
HEAT

P	L	E	R	U	T	A	R	E	P	M	E	T	A
R	W	I	W	R	L	B	O	S	E	V	A	R	U
E	E	L	E	T	E	A	P	O	D	N	O	L	R
C	L	H	C	L	O	S	A	E	O	L	U	R	E
I	H	O	T	U	S	E	V	O	N	J	O	U	L
P	N	E	T	A	H	E	S	K	Y	T	W	C	A
I	E	N	T	Y	E	I	G	H	T	H	X	Q	T
T	A	E	H	O	M	W	A	K	I	G	T	E	I
A	E	M	E	O	O	N	I	W	D	I	N	S	V
T	A	L	U	T	T	E	G	I	I	G	O	E	E
I	S	A	T	U	R	A	T	E	M	R	E	B	H
O	N	A	T	I	N	G	E	L	U	A	H	O	T
N	I	C	S	M	A	R	B	L	H	S	K	O	T

REACHING OUT

What happens if the air is saturated and the temperature drops?

_____

_____

_____

_____

How do we measure relative humidity?

psychrometer [sy-KRAHM-uh-tur]:   instrument that measures relative humidity

LESSON 21 | How do we measure relative humidity?

Have you ever tried air-drying clothes on a humid day? It takes a long time. The air already contains many water molecules. The water from the clothes evaporates very slowly. Evaporate means to turn into a gas.

How fast evaporation takes place depends on the humidity. When the water does evaporate something happens. The surface that had been wet becomes cooler. For example, when the sweat on your body evaporates, your skin cools down.

Now you know two important facts about evaporation. Water evaporates slowly when the air is damp. It evaporates faster when the air is dry. When water evaporates, the temperature goes down.

These facts make it possible to measure relative humidity. Relative humidity is measured with a **psychrometer** [sy-KRAHM-uh-tur]. One kind of psychrometer is the wet-and-dry-bulb thermometer.

A wet-and-dry-bulb thermometer has two thermometers. One of the thermometers has a wet cloth around the bulb. This is the wet bulb. The thermometer without the wet cloth is the dry bulb.

- The dry-bulb thermometer measures the normal air temperature.

- The temperature of the wet-bulb thermometer depends on how fast the water evaporates.

When the air is saturated, no evaporation takes place. The temperature of the wet-bulb thermometer is the same as the dry-bulb thermometer.

When air is not saturated, evaporation does take place. The wet bulb cools down. It has a lower temperature than the dry bulb.

If the wet bulb has a much lower temperature than the dry bulb, it means the air is not very humid.

Figure A shows a wet-and-dry-bulb thermometer. Find the parts listed below. Then write the letter of each part on the correct line.

1. _____ wet-bulb thermometer

   _____ dry-bulb thermometer

   _____ water

   _____ wet cloth

2. What does a wet-and-dry-bulb thermometer measure?

   _____

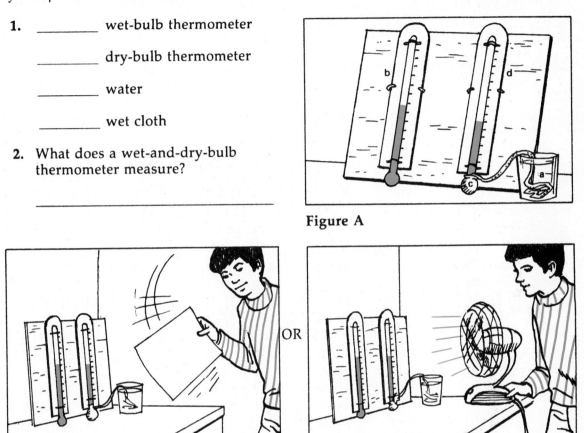

Figure A

OR

Figure B

Figure C

You should fan a wet-and-dry-bulb thermometer before you read the temperatures. This keeps air moving around the wet bulb so that the water evaporates.

You can even spin the thermometers. The psychrometer in Figure D is also called a sling psychrometer [sy-KRAHM-uh-tur].

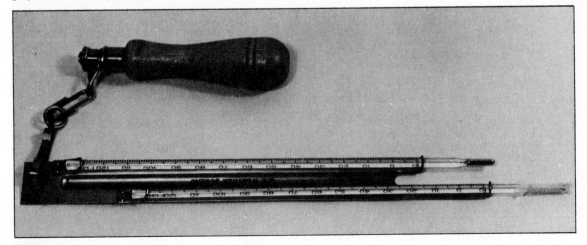

Figure D

In order to find out the relative humidity after you read the temperatures, you must use a chart (Figure E).

1. Find the dry-bulb temperature readings on the chart (column A).

2. Find the temperature difference between the wet and dry thermometers on the chart. (Look on line B).

3. Follow both numbers into the chart. Where the two numbers meet is the percentage relative humidity.

The chart shows one example.

- IF, the dry thermometer reads 80° F and the wet-bulb thermometer reads 75°

- THEN, the temperature difference between the dry and wet thermometers is 5°.

- THEREFORE, the relative humidity is 79%.

RELATIVE HUMIDITY IN PERCENT

Difference in degrees between
wet-bulb and dry-bulb thermometers

(A)	1	2	3	4	5	6	7	8	9	10	11	12	13	14	15	(B)
40°	92	84	76	68	61	53	46	38	31	23	16	9	2			
42°	92	85	77	70	62	55	48	41	34	28	21	14	7			
44°	93	85	78	71	64	57	51	44	37	31	24	18	12	5		
46°	93	86	79	72	65	59	53	46	40	34	28	22	16	10	4	
48°	93	87	80	73	67	60	54	48	42	36	31	25	19	14	8	
50°	93	87	81	74	68	62	56	50	44	39	33	28	22	17	12	
52°	94	88	81	75	69	63	58	52	46	41	36	30	25	20	15	
54°	94	88	82	76	70	65	59	54	48	43	38	33	28	23	18	
56°	94	88	82	77	71	66	61	55	50	45	40	35	31	26	21	
58°	94	89	83	77	72	67	62	57	52	47	42	38	33	28	24	
60°	94	89	84	78	73	68	63	58	53	49	44	40	35	31	27	
62°	94	89	84	79	74	69	64	60	55	50	46	41	37	33	29	
64°	95	90	85	79	75	70	66	61	56	52	48	43	39	35	31	
66°	95	90	85	80	76	71	66	62	58	53	49	45	41	37	33	
68°	95	90	85	81	76	72	67	63	59	55	51	47	43	39	35	
70°	95	90	86	81	77	72	68	64	60	56	52	48	44	40	37	
72°	95	91	86	82	78	73	69	65	61	57	53	49	46	42	39	
74°	95	91	86	82	78	74	70	66	62	58	54	51	47	44	40	
76°	96	91	87	83	78	74	70	67	63	59	55	52	48	45	42	
78°	96	91	87	83	79	75	71	67	64	60	57	53	50	46	43	
80°	96	91	87	83	79	76	72	68	64	61	57	54	51	47	44	
82°	96	91	87	83	79	76	72	69	65	62	58	55	52	49	46	
84°	96	92	88	84	80	77	73	70	66	63	59	56	53	50	47	
86°	96	92	88	84	80	77	73	70	66	63	60	57	54	51	48	
88°	96	92	88	85	81	78	74	71	67	64	61	58	55	52	49	
90°	96	92	88	85	81	78	74	71	68	64	61	58	56	53	50	

Reading of dry-bulb thermometer in degrees of Fahrenheit ———

Figure E

FINDING RELATIVE HUMIDITY

Fill in the missing numbers in the boxes below. Use the chart on the facing page.

	Dry-bulb Temperature °F	Wet-bulb Temperature °F	Temperature Difference	Percentage Relative Humidity
1.	78	73		
2.	54	39		
3.	74	66		
4.	40	29		
5.	90	89		
6.	76	71		
7.	90	75		
8.	62	52		
9.	82	71		
10.	48	37		
11.	80	77		
12.	46	35		

MATCHING

Match each term in Column A with its description in Column B. Write the correct letter in the space provided.

Column A

_____ 1. water vapor

_____ 2. relative humidity

_____ 3. warm air

_____ 4. cold air

_____ 5. psychrometer

Column B

a) the amount of water vapor in the air compared to the amount it can hold at a given temperature

b) can hold little water vapor

c) measures relative humidity

d) can hold a lot of water vapor

e) water in gas form

129

FILL IN THE BLANK

Complete each statement using a term or terms from the list below. Write your answers in the spaces provided.

100%	percent	spin
evaporates	wet-and-dry-bulb thermometer	two
cooler	fan	dry
psychrometer	air temperature	

1. Any instrument that measures relative humidity is called a _____ .

2. The _____ is one kind of psychrometer.

3. A wet-and-dry-bulb thermometer has _____ thermometers.

4. The dry bulb measures _____ .

5. The wet bulb temperature depends on how fast the water _____ .

6. Before we read the temperatures of the wet-and-dry-bulb thermometer, we should

   first _____ or _____ it.

7. Evaporation makes things drier and _____ .

8. Evaporation happens faster when the air is _____ .

9. Relative humidity is written as a _____ .

10. Water does not evaporate when the relative humidity is _____ .

REACHING OUT

Modeling You can make your own wet-and-dry-bulb thermometer. Figure F shows what it should look like. Try and make your own and then show it to your classmates. Be careful when using thermometers.

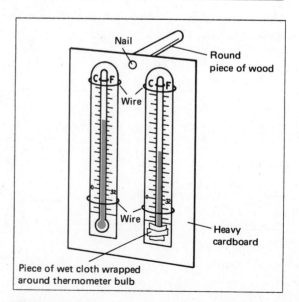

Figure F

How do clouds form?

condensation [kahn-dun-SAY-shun]:   changing of a gas to a liquid
dew point: temperature to which air must be cooled to reach saturation

LESSON 22 | How do clouds form?

You cannot see water vapor. But you can change water vapor into liquid water which you can see.

This is how to do it: Pour some water into a pitcher. Add ice. Let it stand. Soon the pitcher is covered with a thin layer of water. You can see this in Figure B on the facing page.

The water on the outside of the pitcher comes from the air. The cold pitcher cools the air around the pitcher. Now the air can hold less water vapor. In fact, it has more water vapor than it can hold.

The extra water vapor comes out of the air. It changes to liquid water and settles on the pitcher.

The change from a gas to a liquid is called **condensation** [kahn-dun-SAY-shun].

The temperature at which condensation takes place is called the **dew point.**

Now let us use these facts to learn how clouds are formed.

A cloud starts out as moist air. Moist air is lighter than dry air. It rises into the sky.

As the air rises, it cools. When it cools enough, it reaches its dew point. Some of the water vapor in the air condenses. It changes to tiny droplets of water. The water droplets and ice form around dust and other small particles in the air.

These droplets are very light. They are so light that air currents keep them from falling to earth.

As more humid air rises, more water vapor condenses. Little by little, billions and billions of droplets build up. These countless numbers of droplets form what we call a cloud.

Study Figures A and B. Then choose the correct term for each statement. Write your answers in the spaces provided.

Figure A

Figure B

1. The pitcher in Figure B is _____ than the air.

warmer, cooler

2. The pitcher in Figure B _____ the air close to it.

cools, warms

3. The air next to pitcher B now can hold _____ water vapor.

more, less

4. Some water vapor in the air touching this pitcher has _____ .

evaporated, condensed

5. Condensation changes _____ .

a liquid to a gas, a gas to a liquid

6. What do we call the temperature at which condensation takes place?

_____

Match the letters in the diagram with the descriptions. Write the proper letters on the blank lines. Some of these letters may be used more than once.

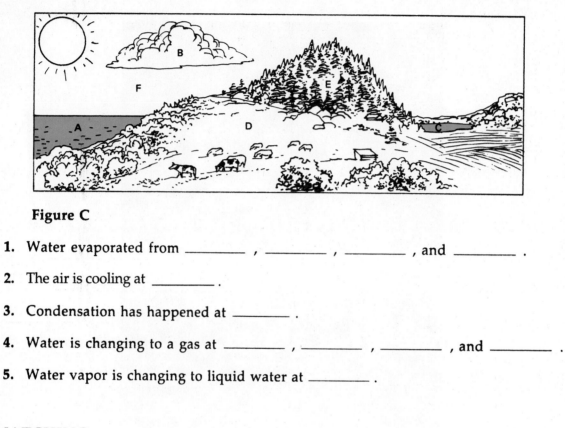

Figure C

1. Water evaporated from _____ , _____ , _____ , and _____ .

2. The air is cooling at _____ .

3. Condensation has happened at _____ .

4. Water is changing to a gas at _____ , _____ , _____ , and _____ .

5. Water vapor is changing to liquid water at _____ .

MATCHING

Match each term in Column A with its description in Column B. Write the correct letter in the space provided.

Column A

_____ 1. evaporation

_____ 2. condensation

_____ 3. dew point

_____ 4. air currents

_____ 5. cloud

Column B

a) the temperature at which a gas changes to a liquid

b) keep droplets from falling

c) the change from a liquid to a gas

d) made up of billions of water droplets

e) the change from a gas to a liquid

Complete each statement using a term or terms from the list below. Write your answers in the spaces provided.

saturated	cloud	more
evaporation	condensation	liquid water
dew point	water vapor	invisible
droplet		

1. Water in the gas form is called ——————— .

2. The change from liquid water to water vapor is called ——————— .

3. Water vapor is ——————— .

4. Warm air can hold ——————— water vapor than cool air can.

5. Air that holds all the water vapor that it can is said to be ——————— .

6. When saturated air cools, extra water vapor changes to ——————— .

7. The change from water vapor to liquid water is called ——————— .

8. The temperature at which condensation takes place is called the ——————— .

9. A very tiny drop is called a ——————— .

10. Many, many billions of droplets make up a ——————— .

TRUE OR FALSE

In the space provided, write "true" if the sentence is true. Write "false" if the sentence is false.

——————— 1. You can always see water.

——————— 2. Water vapor is invisible.

——————— 3. Water vapor is a gas.

——————— 4. Evaporation is the change from a gas to a liquid.

——————— 5. Saturated air cannot hold any more water vapor.

——————— 6. Cold air can hold less water vapor than warm air.

——————— 7. Evaporation happens at the dew point.

——————— 8. When warm air rises, it cools off.

——————— 9. Condensation happens when air cools.

——————— 10. A cloud is made up of water vapor.

Figure D

Everyone has seen dew. We see it on the morning grass. We have seen it cover automobiles.

The sentences below tell how dew is formed. But the sentences are not in the proper order. Rewrite these sentences in proper order on the blank lines below.

1. After the sun goes down, the air and earth cool off.

2. Some water vapor condenses. It changes to drop of dew.

3. During the daytime, the sun evaporates water.

4. The air reaches its dew point.

5. The air becomes moist.

_____

_____

_____

_____

_____

What are the different kinds of clouds?

23

cirrus [SIR-us]:   light, feathery clouds
cumulus [KYOOM-yuh-lus]:   big, puffy clouds
stratus [STRAT-us]:   clouds that form layers across the sky

LESSON 23 | What are the different kinds of clouds?

Can you walk through a cloud? Yes you can! Just take a walk when it is foggy. A fog is one kind of cloud. A fog is a cloud that forms near the ground. Most clouds do not touch the ground. We have to look up into the sky to see them.

Clouds come in many shapes and sizes. Three kinds of clouds you often see are **cumulus** [KYOOM-yuh-lus], **stratus** [STRAT-us], and **cirrus** [SIR-us].

CUMULUS CLOUDS are white and fluffy. They look like large puffs of cotton. Cumulus clouds form mostly on warm summer days. Usually, they mean that the weather will be fair.

In hot weather, a cumulus cloud may grow extra big and turn dark. It becomes a thunderhead.

A thunderhead is a storm cloud. It brings heavy rain with thunder and lightning.

STRATUS CLOUDS are low in the sky. They spread over a large area like a giant gray blanket.

Stratus clouds are rain clouds.

CIRRUS CLOUDS are streaky. They look like thin feathers.

Cirrus clouds are very high in the sky where it is very cold. They are made up of tiny ice crystals.

Cirrus clouds tell us that it may rain or snow within a day or two.

WHAT DO THE CLOUDS SHOW?

Study the pictures of the clouds below. Then answer the questions under the pictures.

Figure A   *Cumulus clouds*

1. What kind of weather do cumulus clouds usually bring? _____

_____

Figure B   *A thunderhead*

2. What kind of weather does a thunderhead bring? _____

_____

Figure C   *Stratus clouds*

3. What kind of weather do stratus clouds bring? _____

_____

Figure D   *Cirrus clouds*

4. What do cirrus clouds tell us may happen? _____

_____

FILL IN THE BLANK

Complete each statement using a term or terms from the list below. Write your answers in the spaces provided. Some words may be used more than once.

ice	droplets of water	cirrus
cumulus	stratus	fog
sizes and shapes	condensed water vapor	

1. A cloud is made up of billions of tiny _____ .

2. The water that makes up clouds comes from _____ .

3. A cloud that is touching the ground is called a _____ .

4. Clouds come in many _____ .

5. Three common kinds of clouds are _____ , _____ , and
_____ clouds.

6. Gray clouds that spread over a large area are called _____ clouds .

7. Feathery-looking clouds are called _____ clouds.

8. Clouds that look like puffs of cotton are called _____ clouds.

9. A thunderhead builds up from a _____ cloud.

10. Cirrus clouds are made up of crystals of _____ .

MATCHING

Match each term in Column A with its description in Column B. Write the correct letter in the space provided.

Column A		Column B	
_____	1. cumulus	a)	low, gray rain clouds
_____	2. stratus	b)	cloud that touches the ground
_____	3. cirrus	c)	storm cloud
_____	4. thunderhead	d)	fair-weather clouds
_____	5. fog	e)	ice clouds

Look at pictures of clouds in Figures E, F, and G. Then answer the questions about the pictures. Write the proper letter on the spaces provided.

Figure E

Which picture . . .

1. shows stratus clouds? _____

2. shows cirrus clouds? _____

3. shows cumulus clouds? _____

Figure F

Which kind of cloud . . .

4. is highest in the sky? _____

5. is lowest in the sky? _____

6. is made up of ice crystals? _____

7. usually mean fair weather? _____

8. means possible rain or snow? _____

9. means rain? _____

10. may become a thunderhead? _____

Figure G

TRUE OR FALSE

In the space provided, write "true" if the sentence is true. Write "false" if the sentence is false.

——————— 1. Clouds are made up of water vapor.

——————— 2. There is only one kind of cloud.

——————— 3. Fog is a cloud.

——————— 4. Stratus clouds are low clouds.

——————— 5. Cumulus clouds mean fair weather.

——————— 6. Stratus clouds are made of ice crystals.

——————— 7. Cirrus clouds are the highest clouds.

——————— 8. A thunderhead builds up from cirrus clouds.

——————— 9. Stratus clouds are rain clouds.

——————— 10. The sizes and shapes of clouds are always changing.

REACHING OUT

We often hear on the weather report that "the fog will burn away." What does that mean?

_____

_____

_____

_____

What is precipitation?

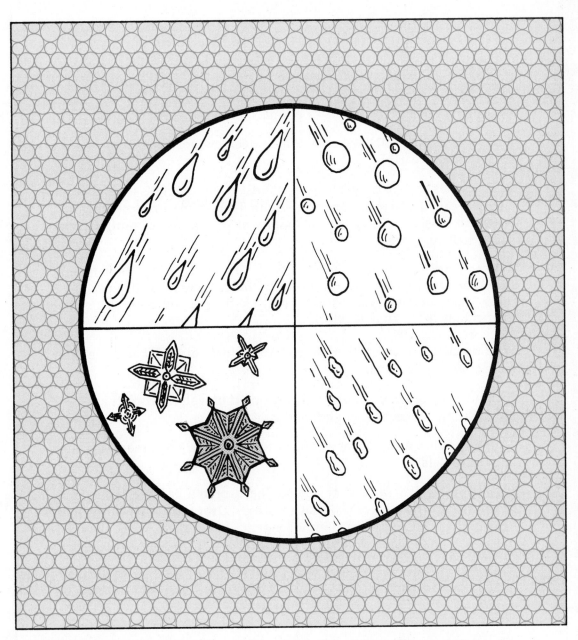

precipitation [prih-sip-uh-TAY-shun]:   water that falls to the earth from the
   atmosphere
rain gauge [GAYJ]:   instrument used to measure precipitation

LESSON 24 | What is precipitation?

Can you imagine our planet without rain? All the water would evaporate. All the oceans, rivers, lakes, and streams would dry up. There would be no water for plants or animals. Nothing could live.

Luckily, this does not happen. Water does evaporate. But, it always comes back to earth!

Water comes back to the earth from clouds. Water that falls to earth from clouds is called **precipitation** [prih-sip-uh-TAY-shun]. Precipitation may be liquid or solid. There are five kinds of precipitation: rain, drizzle, snow, hail, and sleet.

Rain and drizzle are liquid precipitation. They form when the temperature is above freezing. At sea level, the freezing point is 0° C or 32° F. Snow, hail, and sleet are solid precipitation. They form when the temperature is freezing or below.

Why do clouds give up their water? Why does rain fall back to earth? Here is an explanation.

A cloud is made up of billions of tiny droplets of water. Droplets are very light. Rising air keeps them bouncing around.

As they bounce around, the droplets collide. They join up and become larger droplets.

This happens over and over again. The droplets become larger and larger. Finally, they become the size of drops. Drops are much larger and heavier than droplets. Rising air no longer can hold them up. So they fall to earth. Rain is made up of drops. Drizzle is a fine spray of droplets.

Figures A, B, and C show how droplets grow and become drops. Complete the word story below and on the next page by filling in the blank spaces. Choose from the following terms:

over and over again	water	precipitation
cannot	collide	heavier
fall	drops	air currents
light in weight		

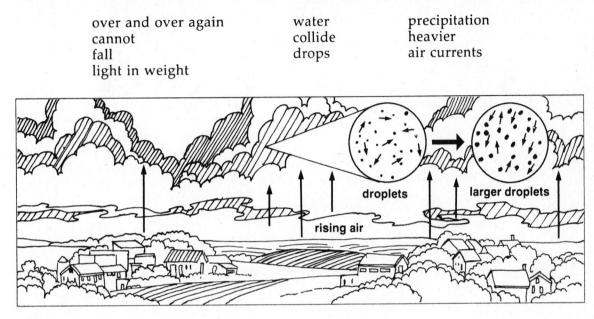

Figure A

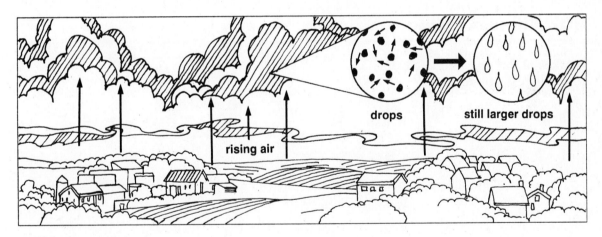

Figure B

1. A cloud is made up of billions of droplets of _____ .

2. Droplets are very _____ .

3. _____ keep them from falling to earth.

4. Moving droplets _____ . They join and become larger droplets.

5. The droplets collide _____ .

6. The droplets become larger and heavier. They become the size of

_____ .

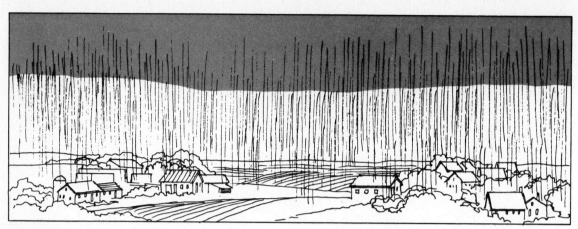

Figure C

7. Drops are much larger and _____ than droplets.

8. Rising air _____ hold them up.

9. The drops _____ to the earth.

10. Water (in liquid or solid form) that falls to earth from clouds is called

    _____ .

HOW BIG IS A DROP?

It takes about one million droplets to make just one drop.

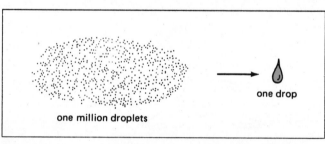

one million droplets

one drop

Figure D

A **rain gauge** [GAYJ] is an instrument that tells us how much it has rained. Rain gauges collect water in one spot.

Rainfall is measured in centimeters or inches.

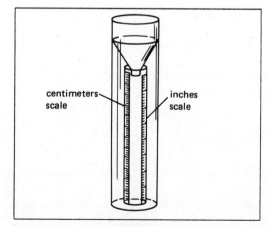

centimeters scale

inches scale

Figure E   *Rain guage*

The graph below shows about how much centimeters of rain fall on some American cities in one year. Study the graph. Then complete the chart below the graph.

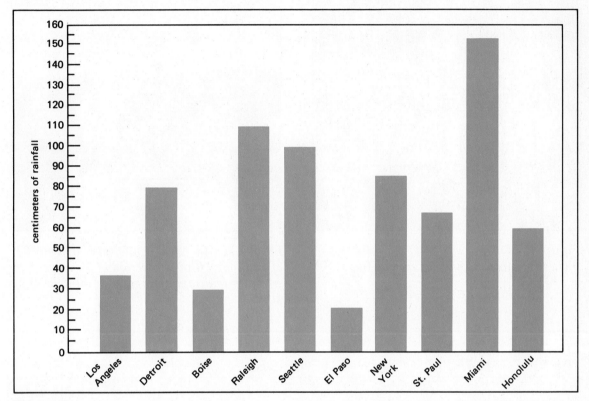

Figure F

	City	Average Yearly Precipitation (Approximate Centimeters)
1.	Boise (Idaho)	
2.	Detroit (Mich.)	
3.	El Paso (Texas)	
4.	Honolulu (Hawaii)	
5.	Los Angeles (Calif.)	
6.	Miami (Florida)	
7.	New York (N.Y.)	
8.	Raleigh (N.C.)	
9.	Seattle (Wash.)	
10.	St. Paul (Minn.)	

THE MOST

THE LEAST

Figure G   *In one year, 2647 cm (1042 inches) of rain fell in Cherrapunji, India.*

Figure H   *In Arica, Chile, just .08 cm (.03 of an inch) fell over a period of 59 years. For 14 years in a row there was no rainfall at all!*

TRUE OR FALSE

In the space provided, write "true" if the sentence is true. Write "false" if the sentence is false.

————————   **1.**   Precipitation comes from clouds.

————————   **2.**   About a million droplets make up a drop.

————————   **3.**   Rain is the only kind of precipitation.

————————   **4.**   Drizzle drops are bigger than raindrops.

————————   **5.**   Sleet is liquid precipitation.

————————   **6.**   Sleet and hail need freezing temperature.

————————   **7.**   A barometer measures rainfall.

————————   **8.**   Rainfall is measured in centimeters and inches.

————————   **9.**   All places get the same amount of precipitation.

————————   **10.**   We can live without precipitation.

Complete each statement using a term or terms from the list below. Write your answers in the spaces provided. Some words may be used more than once.

heavier	hail	below freezing
drizzle	cloud	rising air
drop	above freezing	snow
fall to the ground	rain	larger
sleet	precipitation	

1. A _____ is made up of billions of droplets of water.

2. Droplets are held in the air by _____ .

3. When droplets collide, they become _____ in size.

4. About one million droplets make up a _____ .

5. Drops are much _____ and _____ than droplets.

6. Drops _____ .

7. Water in any form that falls to the earth is called _____ .

8. There are five kinds of precipitation. They are _____ ,

   _____ , _____ , _____ , and

   _____ .

9. It rains or drizzles when the temperature is _____ .

10. It hails, sleets, or snows when the temperature is _____ .

Match each term in Column A with its description in Column B. Write the correct letter in the space provided.

Column A	Column B
_____ 1. precipitation	a) like a fine spray
_____ 2. rain gauge	b) measures rainfall
_____ 3. water vapor	c) change from gas to liquid
_____ 4. condensation	d) any water from the sky
_____ 5. drizzle	e) gas

1. We cannot live without precipitation. Yet, precipitation can cause death and

   suffering. Explain. _____

   _____

   _____

   _____

   _____

2. How would you measure snowfall? _____

   _____

   _____

   _____

How do snow, sleet, and hail form?

LESSON 25 | How do snow, sleet, and hail form?

Did you ever pack a snowball or make a snowman?

You cannot shape rain because rain is a liquid. Snow is different. Snow is a solid. It has a shape of its own. And we can change the shape of snow after it reaches the ground.

Snow is one kind of solid precipitation. There are two other kinds, sleet and hail. Each one forms in a different way. Let us study each one.

SNOW Water vapor condenses to form clouds. If the temperature around the clouds is <u>above</u> freezing, the vapor changes to <u>liquid</u> droplets.

If, however, the temperature around the clouds is freezing, the vapor changes to tiny snow crystals.

The tiny snow crystals grow and grow. When they become heavy enough, they fall to earth. It snows.

SLEET Sleet is made of frozen raindrops.

Sometimes it is colder near the ground than it is up in the clouds. Rain falls from the clouds and goes through a layer of very cold air before hitting the ground. This makes the raindrops freeze. The frozen raindrops fall to the earth as sleet.

HAIL Hail forms during some thunderstorms.

Strong air currents keep the raindrops moving in the air for a long time. As they move, they pass through many cold and warm layers of air.

In the cold air, the raindrops freeze. They change to icy beads. In the warm air, more water builds up around the beads. Then the water freezes when they pass through another cold layer.

This happens over and over again. Each time the icy beads become bigger. They become hailstones and fall to earth.

Figure A *Rain*

Figure A shows rain falling.

1. The temperature around the clouds

   is _____ freezing.
      above, below

2. The temperature near the ground is

   _____ freezing.
      above, below

Figure B *Sleet*

Figure B shows sleet hitting the ground.

3. Sleet starts out as _____ .
                         ice, rain

4. The temperature around the clouds

   is _____ freezing.
      above, below

5. The temperature near the ground is

   _____ freezing.
      above, below

Figure C shows freshly fallen snow.

6. The temperature around the clouds

   is _____ freezing.
      above, below

7. Tiny snow _____ grow
                drops, crystals

   until they fall to earth.

Figure C *Snow*

Figure D

Figure D shows how hail grows. Trace it step by step.

8. At A, the precipitation is _____ .
   <u>a liquid, a solid</u>

9. Air currents push it up to B. At B, it _____ .
   <u>changes to ice, is still a liquid</u>

10. The ice drops to C. At C _____ .
    <u>more ice forms, water builds around the ice</u>

11. Rising air pushes the ice up to D. At D the _____ .
    <u>added water freezes, ice melts</u>

12. The ice becomes _____ .
    <u>smaller, bigger</u>

13. At E, the "bead" of ice is falling to earth. What has it become? _____

FILL IN THE BLANK

Complete each statement using a term or terms from the list below. Write your answers in the spaces provided.

| solid | below | precipitation |
| freezing | liquid | |

1. Any form of water that falls from clouds is called _____ .

2. Rain and drizzle are precipitation in the _____ state.

3. Snow, sleet, and hail are precipitation in the _____ state.

4. Rain and drizzle form in temperatures that are _____ freezing.

5. Snow, sleet, and hail form in _____ temperatures.

154

MATCHING

Match each term in Column A with its description in Column B. Write the correct letter in the space provided.

Column A	Column B
_____ 1. water vapor	a) built-up ice beads
_____ 2. condensation	b) frozen raindrops
_____ 3. snow	c) change from gas to liquid
_____ 4. sleet	d) falls as flakes
_____ 5. hail	e) water in the gas form

SOME INTERESTING FACTS ABOUT SNOW AND HAIL

In the continental United States, the most snow falls in some places in California.

Figure E *152 centimeters (60 inches) fell in just one day in a place called Giant Forest.*

Figure F *2245 centimeters (884 inches) fell in just one winter at Tamarach, California (1906-7). That's more than 22 meters (73 feet).*

Figure G

Every snowflake has six sides or six points. BUT—no two snowflakes are exactly alike. Can you imagine how many snowflakes have fall since the earth was formed? **Each one was different.**

Figure H

Hailstones come in many sizes. They can be very big. Some are as large as marbles. Sometimes they are bigger than baseballs.

The largest hailstones fell in 1928 at Potter, Nebraska. They measured 43 centimeters (17 inches) around, and weighed .68 kilometers (1 1/2 pounds).

Figure I   *Hail does a lot of damage in some parts of our country. It destroys crops and kills cattle.*

What is an air mass?

26

air mass: large area of air that has the same temperature and amount of moisture
continental [KAHNT-un-ent-ul] **air mass:** air mass that forms over land
maritime [MAR-ih-tym] **air mass:** air mass that forms over oceans
polar air mass: air mass that forms over cold regions
tropical [TRAHP-ih-kul] **air mass:** air mass that forms over warm regions

LESSON 26 | What is an air mass?

What will the weather be tomorrow? Is rain on the way? Will sunny weather be moving in?

Weather moves from place to place. But where does it come from? Where does weather start?

Most weather comes from **air masses.** An air mass is a huge body of air. It covers a very large area. Places within this area have about the same temperature and humidity, or amount of moisture.

An air mass starts over the ocean or over a large body of land. The air that makes up an air mass stalls over the water or land. It stands still for several days or weeks. During this time, the land or water gives the air its temperature and humidity. The air mass then moves on.

The <u>humidity</u> of air masses depends on where they form.

• Air masses that form over the ocean are called **maritime** [MAR-ih-tym] **air masses.** Maritime air is moist.

• Air masses that form over the land are called **continental** [KAHNT-un-ent-ul] **air masses.** Continental air is dry.

The <u>temperature</u> of air masses also depends on where they form.

• Air masses that form near the poles are called **polar air masses.**

• Air masses that form near the tropics are called **tropical** [TRAHP-ih-kul] **air masses.** Tropical air is warm.

The name of an air mass has two parts:

• The first part tells us that it is either maritime or continental.

• The second part tells that it is either tropical or polar.

For example, the name <u>continental tropical</u> tells us that the air mass formed over tropical land. The air would be dry and warm.

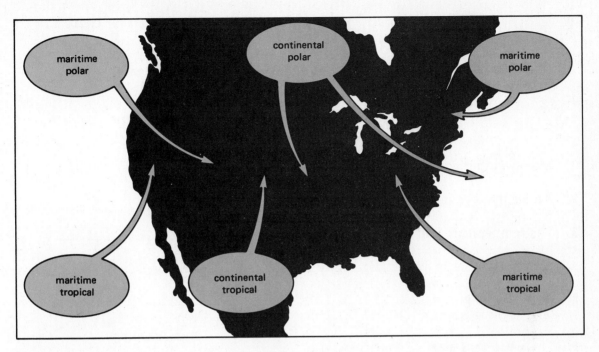

Figure A

The map (Figure A) shows the air masses that bring weather to North America. Study the map carefully. Then answer these questions.

1. Name the four kinds of air masses this map shows:

   _____   _____

   _____   _____

2. Which of these air masses move in from:

   a) the north? _____

   b) the south? _____

   c) the land? _____

   d) the ocean? _____

3. Which air mass brings

   a) cold and dry air? _____

   b) warm and dry air? _____

4. Which air masses bring

   a) cold and moist air? _____

   b) warm and moist air? _____

FILL IN THE BLANK

Complete each statement using a term or terms from the list below. Write your answers in the spaces provided.

very large area	moist	water
humidity	air masses	cold
warm	continental	the same
land	temperature	maritime

1. Most weather comes from _____ .

2. An air mass covers a _____ .

3. The temperature and humidity in an air mass stay about _____ .

4. An air mass starts over a large body of _____ or _____ .

5. An air mass gets its _____ and _____ from the water or land it came from.

6. The word that means "water" is _____ .

7. The word that means "land" is _____ .

8. The temperature of air that comes from the tropics is very _____ .

9. The temperature of air that comes from the poles is very _____ .

10. Air that comes from over the ocean is very _____ .

MATCHING

Match each term in Column A with its description in Column B. Write the correct letter in the space provided.

Column A		Column B	
_____	1. maritime polar	a)	dry and warm
_____	2. continental tropical	b)	moist and warm
_____	3. continental polar	c)	moist and cold
_____	4. maritime tropical	d)	dry and cold
_____	5. humidity	e)	amount of moisture

What happens when air masses meet?

front: surface between different air masses

warm front: forward edge of a warm air mass formed when a warm air mass pushes over a cold air mass

Warm and cold air masses do not mix. When warm and cold air masses meet, they collide. The masses "battle" each other. The meeting causes many weather changes.

The boundary between two air masses is called a **front.** One kind of front is called a **warm front.**

A WARM FRONT FORMS WHEN A MOVING WARM AIR MASS PUSHES AGAINST A COLD AIR MASS.

The warm air of the front pushes upward. It flows over the top of the cooler air mass.

Many clouds form along a warm front. They may reach out for 1600 kilometers (1000 miles) or more.

At first there are only thin cirrus clouds high in the sky. Then stratus clouds move in. Slowly, the clouds become lower and lower. The sky becomes darker and darker. Finally, it rains.

Precipitation along a warm front is even and steady. It keeps falling until the front passes. It may last a few days. Then the weather becomes clearer and warmer. A warm air mass has moved in.

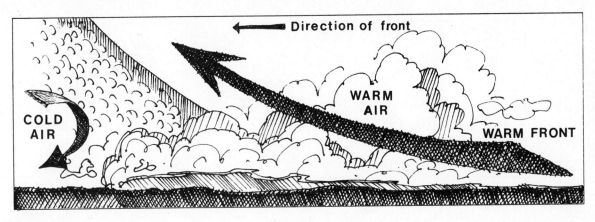

Figure A

Figure A shows a warm front. Find the two air masses. The warm air pushes upward and flows over the cold air. Many clouds form where the two air masses meet.

See for yourself how a warm front brings weather changes slowly.

What To Do

1. Get a thin piece of paper. Tracing paper would be best.

2. Put your paper over Figure B and trace it.

3. Now put the traced drawing over Figure C, lining up the x's.

4. Slowly, move the tracing to the right until the y's match up. Now, imagine yourself to be at spot y. What would you see? What would you feel?

Figure B

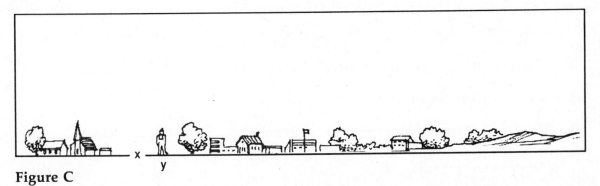

Figure C

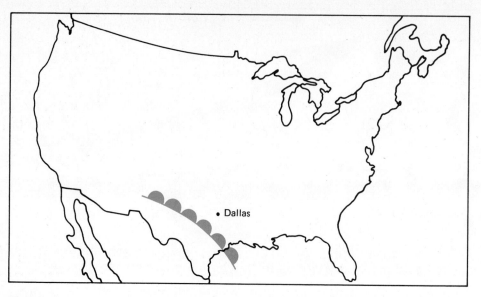

Figure D

The symbol for a warm front is ▬▬▬▬▬ . Figure D shows what it looks like on a weather map. The warm front on this map is moving towards Dallas. Its speed is about 24 kilometers (15 miles) per hour. Dallas is 240 kilometers away.

In how many hours will the warm front reach Dallas? _____

FILL IN THE BLANK

Complete each statement using a term or terms from the list below. Write your answers in the spaces provided.

darker	boundary	"battle each other"
weather changes	lower	clearer and warmer
front passes	warm front	clouds
rain	maps	

1. A front is the _____ between two air masses.

2. When warm air and cold air meet, they _____ .

3. A front brings about _____ .

4. A warm air mass that pushes a cold air mass is called a _____ .

5. A warm front forms many _____ .

6. The clouds along a warm front slowly become _____ and

    _____ .

164

7. A warm front brings steady _____ .

8. Precipitation along a warm front continues until the _____ .

9. After a warm front passes, the weather becomes _____ .

10. The symbol for a warm front (🌡🌡🌡🌡🌡) is shown on weather

_____ .

FIND THE PARTS

Figure E shows a warm front. Find the parts listed below. Write the correct letter in the spaces provided. Then fill in the blanks.

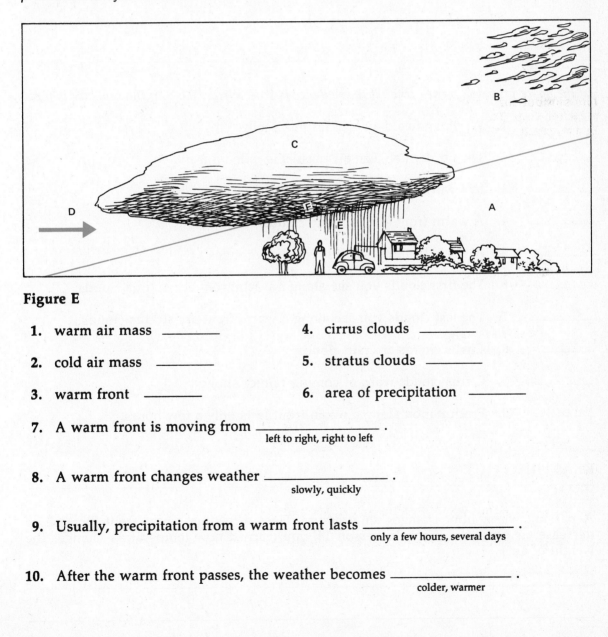

Figure E

1. warm air mass _____

2. cold air mass _____

3. warm front _____

4. cirrus clouds _____

5. stratus clouds _____

6. area of precipitation _____

7. A warm front is moving from _____ .

left to right, right to left

8. A warm front changes weather _____ .

slowly, quickly

9. Usually, precipitation from a warm front lasts _____ .

only a few hours, several days

10. After the warm front passes, the weather becomes _____ .

colder, warmer

MATCHING

Match each term in Column A with its description in Column B. Write the correct letter in the space provided.

	Column A		Column B
_____	1. warm front	a)	boundary between two air masses
_____	2. cold air and warm air	b)	kinds of precipitation
_____	3. ▰▰▰▰▰▰▰	c)	pushes against a cold air mass
_____	4. rain and snow	d)	do not mix easily
_____	5. front	e)	warm front symbol

TRUE OR FALSE

In the space provided, write "true" if the sentence is true. Write "false" if the sentence is false.

_____ 1. Warm and cold air masses mix easily.

_____ 2. The border between air masses is called a front.

_____ 3. In a warm front, warm air pushes against cold air.

_____ 4. A warm front brings many clouds.

_____ 5. A warm front causes fast weather changes.

_____ 6. The first clouds you see along a warm front are stratus clouds.

_____ 7. The last clouds you see along a warm front are stratus clouds.

_____ 8. Cirrus clouds are rain clouds.

_____ 9. Cirrus clouds warn of coming rain or snow.

_____ 10. Precipitation along a warm front lasts only a few hours.

REACHING OUT

A passing warm front changes air pressure. Does a passing warm front increase or decrease air pressure? (Hint: In Lesson 14, you learned how temperature changes the weight of air.)

_____

_____

What are some other kinds of fronts?

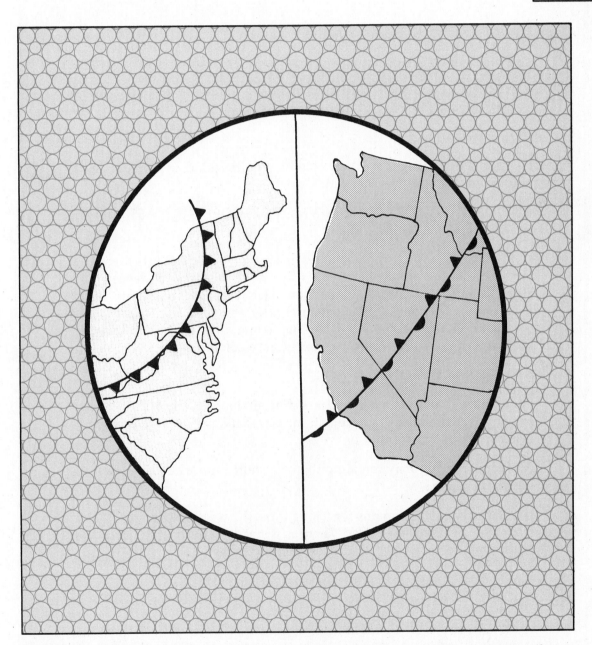

cold front: forward edge of a cold air mass, formed when a cold air mass pushes under a warm air mass

stationary [STAY-shuh-ner-ee] **front:** boundary between two unlike air masses where there is little movement of air

LESSON 28 | What are some other kinds of fronts?

Warm fronts are not the only kind of fronts. There are also **cold fronts** and **stationary** [STAY-shuh-ner-ee] **fronts.**

COLD FRONT

A warm front changes weather slowly. Another kind of front, called **a cold front,** changes weather quickly.

A COLD FRONT FORMS WHEN A MOVING COLD AIR MASS PUSHES AGAINST A WARM AIR MASS.

A moving cold front "scoops up" warm air that it meets. It lifts the warm air high into the atmosphere. The warm air cools and condenses. Tall storm clouds form. Strong winds blow. Heavy rain or snow falls. But it lasts only a few hours. A short time after the cold front passes, the weather becomes clearer and drier. The temperature drops suddenly. In the wintertime, a cold front may bring very cold air.

STATIONARY FRONT

Sometimes a cold air mass and a warm air mass meet, but then stop moving. The boundary between air masses that have stopped moving is called a stationary front.

A stationary front may remain only for a short time. Then there is little weather change.

If a stationary front remains for a long time, the weather changes. Warm front-like weather takes over. There is a steady rain. It may last a few days. Then the sky clears and it becomes warmer.

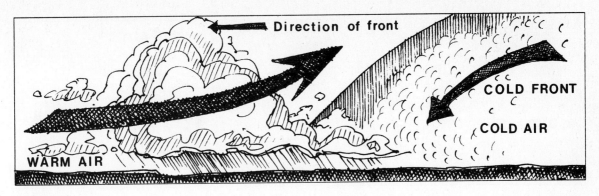

Figure A

Figure A shows a cold front. Find the two air masses. The moving cold air pushes the warm air high up. Many storm clouds form.

A cold front brings rapid weather changes.

What To Do

1. Get a thin piece of paper. Tracing paper would be best.

2. Put your paper over Figure B and trace it.

3. Now put the traced drawing over Figure C, lining up the x's.

4. Slowly, move the tracing to the right over Figure C until the y's match up.

Now imagine yourself to be at spot y. What would you see? What would you feel?

Figure B

Figure C

WHAT A STATIONARY FRONT LOOKS LIKE

Figure D

Figure D shows a stationary front. A stationary front brings very little change in the weather.

MORE WEATHER MAP SYMBOLS

The symbol for a cold front is ▲▲▲▲▲ .

The symbol for a stationary front is ▼●▼●▼ .

Figure E shows what these symbols look like on a weather map.

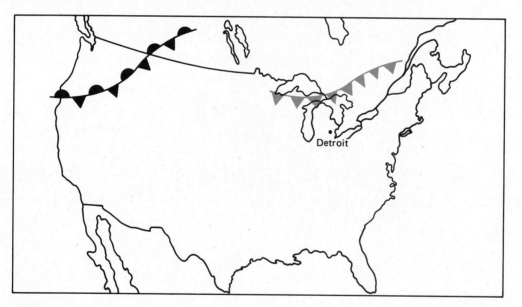

Figure E

The cold front on this map is moving towards Detroit. Its speed is about 40 kilometers (25 miles) per hour. Detroit is 440 kilometers away.

In how many hours will the cold front reach Detroit? _____

FILL IN THE BLANK

Complete each statement using a term or terms from the list below. Write your answers in the spaces provided.

storm clouds   does not
for a long time   stationary front
cold front

1. When a cold air mass pushes against a warm air mass, a _____ is formed.

2. A cold front produces big _____ .

3. Precipitation from cold front clouds _____ last a long time.

4. The border between "stalled" air masses is called a _____ .

5. Warm-front weather follows if a stationary front remains _____ .

FIND THE PARTS

Figure F shows a cold front. Find the parts listed below. Write the correct letter in the spaces provided. Then fill in the blanks.

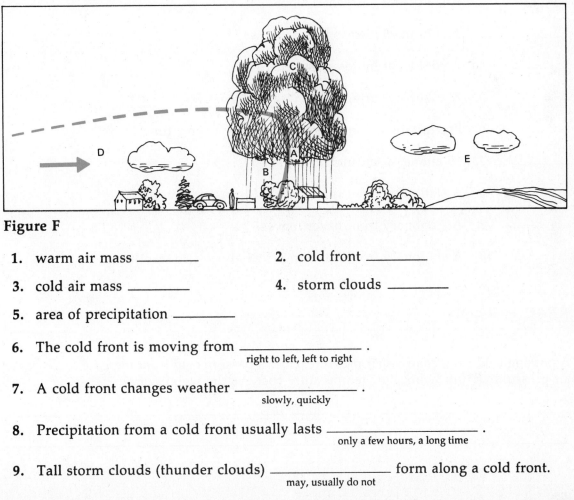

Figure F

1. warm air mass _____

2. cold front _____

3. cold air mass _____

4. storm clouds _____

5. area of precipitation _____

6. The cold front is moving from _____ .
   <u>right to left, left to right</u>

7. A cold front changes weather _____ .
   <u>slowly, quickly</u>

8. Precipitation from a cold front usually lasts _____ .
   <u>only a few hours, a long time</u>

9. Tall storm clouds (thunder clouds) _____ form along a cold front.
   <u>may, usually do not</u>

MATCHING

Match each term in Column A with its description in Column B. Write the correct letter in the space provided.

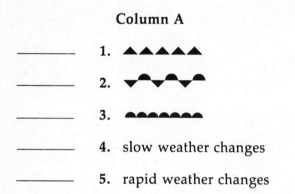

	Column A		Column B
_____	1. ▲▲▲▲▲	a)	symbol for a stationary front
_____	2. ▼◠▼◠▼◠	b)	caused by a warm front
_____	3. ◠◠◠◠◠	c)	symbol for a cold front
_____	4. slow weather changes	d)	caused by a cold front
_____	5. rapid weather changes	e)	symbol for a warm front

TRUE OR FALSE

In the space provided, write "true" if the sentence is true. Write "false" if the sentence is false.

_____ 1. A moving cold front moves cold air over warm air.

_____ 2. A cold front has gentle slope.

_____ 3. A cold front always brings snow.

_____ 4. A cold front builds storm clouds.

_____ 5. A cold front brings slow weather changes.

_____ 6. Precipitation along a cold front lasts a short time.

_____ 7. "Stationary" means moving.

_____ 8. A stationary front is a front that is not moving.

_____ 9. A stationary front never moves.

_____ 10. A stationary front can bring clear and warm weather.

REACHING OUT

A passing cold front changes air pressure. Does a passing cold front increase or decrease air pressure? (Hint: Think how temperature changes the weight of air.)

_____

_____

What are thunderstorms, hurricanes, and tornados? | 29

hurricane [hur-uh-KAYN]:   tropical storm with very strong winds
thunderstorm: storm with thunder, lightning, heavy rain, and strong winds
tornado [tohr-NAY-doh]:   small, very violent funnel-shaped storm

LESSON 29 | What are thunderstorms, hurricanes, and tornados?

Does the booming sound of loud thunder scare you? A thunderstorm is one kind of severe storm. Hurricanes [hur-uh-KAYNS] and tornados [tor-NAY-dohs] also are severe storms. Now let us learn about each one.

THUNDERSTORMS   A **thunderstorm** is a storm with thunder, lightning, heavy rain, and strong winds. Thunderstorms usually happen when a cold front and a warm front meet. They start when huge cumulus clouds form giant storm clouds. Lightning is caused when giant storm clouds give off electricity. The electricity causes the air to warm and expand quickly. Thunder is caused by the expanding and contracting air. But did you ever notice that you see lightning before you hear thunder? That is because light moves faster than sound.

HURRICANES   Sometimes a very low-pressure area forms over the ocean near the equator. A tropical air mass picks up a lot of moisture from the warm waters. Such low pressure causes very strong winds and heavy rain. When such a powerful storm forms over an ocean, it is called a **hurricane.**

A hurricane moves in a wide circular path. From an airplane, it looks like bands of spinning clouds. The winds spiral toward the center of the storm. The center is called the eye of the storm. Does it surprise you that the eye is calm and clear? Sometimes it reaches land and causes much destruction. Winds can reach close to 325 kilometers per hour (200 mph). Rains can cause flooding.

In 1969, hurricane Camille killed almost 300 people in the southern United States. It caused about half a billion dollars worth of damage to property. A similar storm (called a typhoon) in Bangladesh killed almost half a million people in 1970.

TORNADOS   The most violent kind of storm is a **tornado.** It looks like a dark, curving funnel reaching down from a black cloud. It is a small storm and lasts only a short time. But in its path it causes tremendous destruction.

Its low pressure causes winds up to 800 kilometers per hour (500 mph). It blows down buildings and trees. It tumbles automobiles and trucks. It often picks up and carries people hundreds of feet.

The worst tornado in history happened March 18, 1925. This "twister" was much larger and faster than most. It killed 689 people as it roared across parts of Missouri, Illinois, and Indiana.

Figure A

Would you want to fly directly into a hurricane? That is what some hurricane hunters do! Hurricane hunters often take pictures of hurricanes. They fly over the hurricane and take the pictures. Hurricane hunters who fly into the storm gather information for the National Weather Service.

Figure B

Figure C

Tornados occur in many parts of the world. However, more tornados occur in the United States than anywhere else. During some years, there are more than 800 tornados.

Oklahoma and Kansas have more tornados than any other states. Most of these tornados form in the Great Plains and the southwestern United States. This area is called the "Tornado Belt" or "Tornado Alley."

Most tornados in the "Tornado Belt" happen during April, May, and June. They usually strike during the late afternoon. These are the times when conditions are best for tornados to form.

The National Weather Service warns people when hurricanes or tornados are coming.

During a hurricane, people are told to tape their windows with large "X"s from corner to corner.

During a tornado, people are advised to take shelter in a basement.

Figure D

TRUE OR FALSE

In the space provided, write "true" if the sentence is true. Write "false" if the sentence is false.

_____ **1.** Thunderstorms usually happen when a cold front and a warm front meet.

_____ **2.** Thunder is caused by the expanding and contracting of air.

_____ **3.** Tornados last a long time.

_____ **4.** Sound travels faster than light.

_____ **5.** Powerful storms that form over the oceans are called typhoons.

_____ **6.** A hurricane moves in a wide circular path.

_____ **7.** Oklahoma and Kansas have more tornados than any other states.

_____ **8.** Thunderstorms begin when huge cumulus clouds form.

_____ **9.** A hurricane is an area of very high pressure.

_____ **10.** A tornado is a small funnel-shaped cloud that spins.

COMPLETE THE CHART

Decide whether each characteristic listed in the table belongs to a hurricane, a thunderstorm, or a tornado. Place a check mark in the correct column.

	Characteristic	Hurricane	Thunderstorm	Tornado
1.	Funnel-shaped cloud			
2.	Lightning			
3.	Calm and clear eye			
4.	Cold front and warm front meet			
5.	Winds spiral toward center			
6.	Very small			
7.	Forms during late spring			
8.	Huge cumulus clouds			
9.	Clouds give off electricity			
10.	Looks like bands of spinning clouds			
11.	Acts like giant vacuum cleaner			
12.	Loud noise caused by expanding and contracting air			

NOW TRY THIS

Answer the questions below about severe storms.

1. What are two characteristics of thunderstorms?

   _____

2. What are two characteristics of tornados?

   _____

3. What are two characteristics of hurricanes?

   _____

4. Sketch a picture of a tornado cloud in the space provided.

SCIENCE *EXTRA*

Meteorologist

An airplane pilot is mapping out a course to a distant city. The pilot needs to know the wind speed and direction, visibility, and cloud conditions that may be present on the flight path. The pilot depends on weather information gathered by meteorologists [meet-ee-uh-RAHL-uh-jists].

Meteorologists are scientists who study the atmosphere and how it behaves. They try to understand and predict the weather. Meteorologists gather information about the atmosphere at hundreds of different places and at many altitudes. Meteorologists also study changing global weather and the effects of air pollution on the weather.

Modern day meteorologists use many tools and instruments to compile weather statistics. Tools such as weather satellites and computers are used by meteorologists to gather information. Meteorologists are interested in the amount of precipitation in an area, the pressure of the atmosphere, wind speeds, and cloud formation. They also gather weather information about wind patterns and ocean currents. All of the information gathered by meteorologists is then sent to the National Oceanic and Atmospheric Administration, where weather maps are produced.

Meteorologists are employed by the National Weather Service, airlines and airports, news bureaus, and groups of farmers. The weather forecaster on the evening news is a meteorologist. Other meteorologists are employed by the military.

Weather forecasting is only one part of being a meteorologist. Meteorologists work at weather stations where they record data and make observations.

To become a meteorologist, you should be a careful observer, and be a detail oriented person. During high school, you should take courses in science and mathematics. Training in meteorology can be obtained from a community college or technical school. For a more advanced job in meteorology, a college education is necessary.

How can you find out about weather?

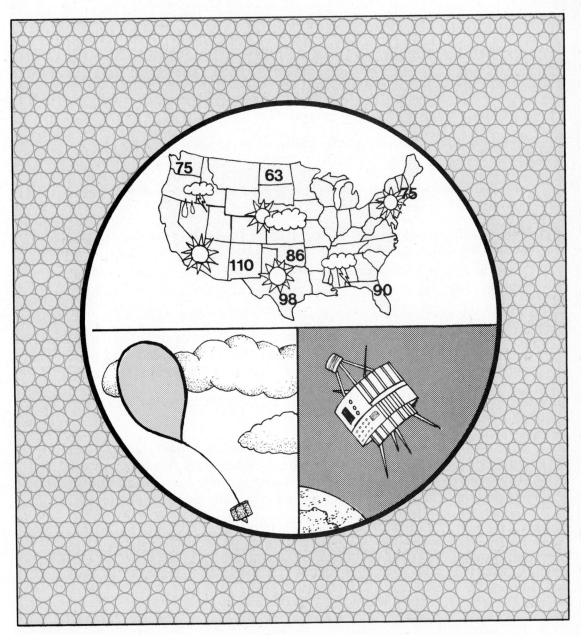

meteorologist [meet-ee-uhr-AHL-uh-jist]:   person who studies weather
station model: record of weather information at a weather station

LESSON 30 | How can you find out about weather?

You stand at your window and look outside. The sky is gray. It's raining "cats and dogs." Yet, the weather report predicts sunny weather. It does not seem possible!

A little time passes and, sure enough, the sky starts to clear. Soon, the sun breaks through. It is a beautiful day! The weather reporter's prediction has come true.

How does the weather reporter know what the weather will be?

Predicting weather is not a simple job. It takes teamwork by hundreds of weather scientists. A weather scientist is called a **meteorologist** [meet-ee-uhr-AHL-uh-jist].

Many meteorologists work for the United States Weather Service. The Weather Service has more than 600 weather stations. They are spread over the country. Some are even outside the country. Each station has all the weather instruments, such as weather balloons and weather satellites.

The meteorologists read the instruments four times a day. They mark down the temperature, humidity, air pressure, wind speed, and wind direction. If there is any rain or snow they mark that down, too.

The weather scientists also look at the sky. They mark down the kind of clouds they see and how high they are.

All this data is put into a number code. It is sent to a main station. Here, the data is put on a master map. The data describes the air masses in different places. By knowing how fast and in what direction air masses are moving, meteorologists can make predictions. Sometimes, computers help them make predictions.

Weather predictions are not always right. But they are right about 80 to 90 percent of the time. And that is a pretty good record!

Not all weather data comes from weather stations. The picture chart below shows other sources of weather date. It also shows what happens to the data after it is collected.

weather stations   weather balloons   weather satellites

Main weather office gathers the data

radar   airplanes and ships at sea

The data is placed on a map . . . weather predictions are made

Predictions are sent to many places. They include newspapers, radio stations, and television stations.

Figure A shows what the data from a weather station looks like.

It is called a **station model.**

The number code and symbols are a short-cut way of writing the data.

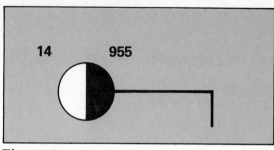

Figure A

Station models from the hundreds of weather stations are used to make a map like Figure B.

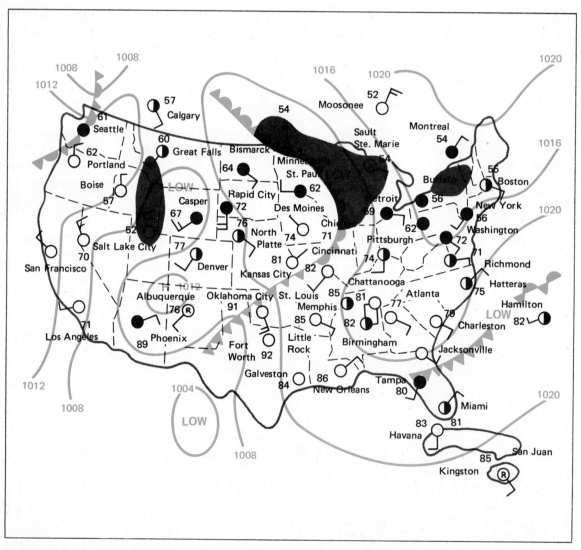

Figure B

Get ready for a surprise! In the next Lessons you will be making maps like this!

FILL IN THE BLANK

Complete each statement using a term or terms from the list below. Write your answers in the spaces provided.

predict weather   station model   radar
meteorologist   weather balloons   U.S. Weather Service
weather satellites   four times a day   code
six hundred   weather map   weather instruments
airplanes and ships

1. A weather scientist is called a _____ .

2. In the United States, gathering weather data and predicting weather is the job of the

   _____ .

3. The Weather Service operates more than _____ weather stations.

4. Every weather station has _____ .

5. Weather station instruments are checked _____ .

6. Weather data is sent to a main station in _____ form.

7. The data from a single weather station is called a _____ .

8. Meteorologists use all the station models to make a master _____ .

9. A weather map helps us to _____ .

10. Much weather data comes from weather stations. Weather data also comes from

    _____ , _____ , _____ ,

    and _____ .

MATCHING

Match each term in Column A with its description in Column B. Write the correct letter in the space provided.

Column A

_____ 1. meteorologist

_____ 2. barometer

_____ 3. station model

_____ 4. more than 600

_____ 5. NE, 25 kilometers per hour

Column B

a) weather data from a single station

b) number of U.S. Weather Stations

c) a weather instrument

d) example of weather data

e) weather scientist

TRUE OR FALSE

In the space provided, write "true" if the sentence is true. Write "false" if the sentence is false.

———————— 1. A weather scientist is called a meteor.

———————— 2. Only a meteorologist can predict weather.

———————— 3. You can learn to predict weather.

———————— 4. Predicting weather in the United States is the job mainly of the U.S. Weather Service.

———————— 5. There are 60 U.S. Weather Service weather stations.

———————— 6. U.S. Weather Service stations are only in the United States.

———————— 7. Some weather information comes from ships at sea, airplanes, satellites, and radar.

———————— 8. In a way, your eyes can be called weather instruments.

———————— 9. A weather station gets its information only from instruments.

———————— 10. Most weather predictions are correct.

REACHING OUT

Why do you think weather predictions are becoming more and more accurate?

——

——

——

——

——

What is an isobar?

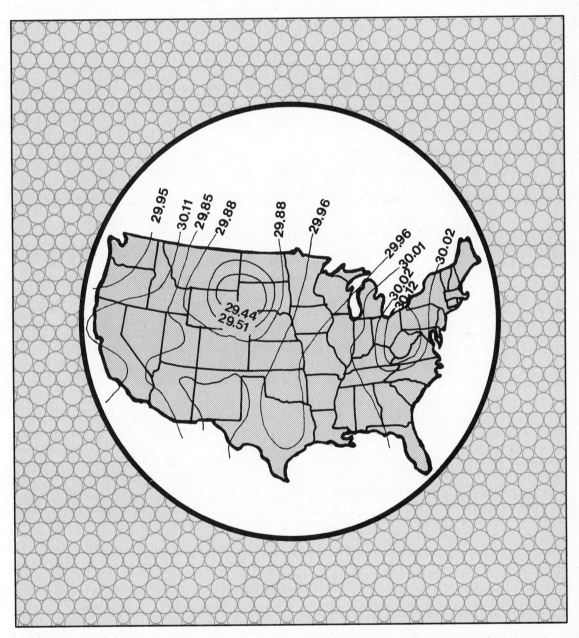

isobar [Y-suh-bar]: line on a weather map that connects points of equal pressure
millibars [MIL-uh-bahrz]: unit of measurement for air pressure

LESSON 31 | What is an isobar?

A weather map shows us weather conditions from many places. How is air pressure shown on a map?

Air pressure is measured in units called **millibars** [MIL-uh-bahrz]. The numbers in Figures A, C, and D on the following pages are in millibars.

An **isobar** [Y-suh-bar] is a special line on a weather map. It joins places that have the same air pressure. Notice how the numbers in Figures A and C are joined by isobars. An isobar follows a curved path. The ends meet to form a closed figure.

Look at the isobars in the west in Figure C. The numbers become larger toward the center. The isobars show a high-pressure area.

Dry air weighs more than moist air. The more the air weighs, the higher the pressure is. Weather in a high-pressure area is generally dry and fair. A high-pressure area is shown with an "H" in the center of the pressure area.

Now look at the isobars in the east in Figure C. The numbers become smaller toward the center. The isobars show a low-pressure area.

Moist air weighs less than dry air. The less the air weighs, the lower the pressure is. The weather in a low-pressure area is generally cloudy or rainy. A low-pressure area is shown with an "L" in the center of the pressure area.

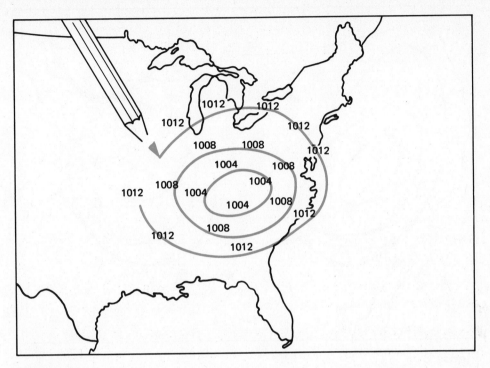

Figure A

FIRST, mark the air pressure readings on the map. (The numerals stand for millibars.)

THEN, draw a line through places of equal pressure. (They have the same millibar numerals.)

1. How many isobars does Figure A have? _____

2. a) How many different pressure numbers are shown? _____

   List them. _____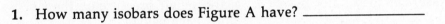

   _____

   _____

   b) Which number shows the highest pressure? _____

   c) Which number shows the lowest pressure? _____

3. Mark the kind of pressure area on Figure A.

4. What is an isobar? _____

5. Name the instrument that measures air pressure. _____
   (Look back to Lesson 13 if you have to.)

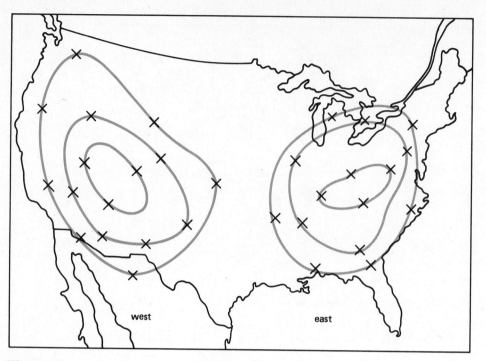

Figure B

Figure B shows two large pressure areas. One is in the east; the other in the west. Each pressure area has three isobars. There are x's along each isobar.

WEST

1. Mark the air pressure on the x's along each isobar.

   Start with the outside isobar.

   > 1022 millibars
   > 1026 millibars
   > 1030 millibars

   Now answer these questions.

2. As you go towards the center, the

   pressure becomes _____ .
   greater, lower

3. This is a _____ pressure
   high, low

   area. Label it in the proper way.

4. The weather in this area is probably

   _____ .
   fair, cloudy

EAST

5. Mark the air pressure on the x's along each isobar.

   Start with the outside isobar.

   > 1008 millibars
   > 1004 millibars
   > 1000 millibars

   Now answer these questions.

6. As you go towards the center, the

   pressure becomes _____ .
   greater, lower

7. This is a _____ pressure
   high, low

   area. Label it in the proper way.

8. The weather in this area is probably

   _____ .
   fair, cloudy

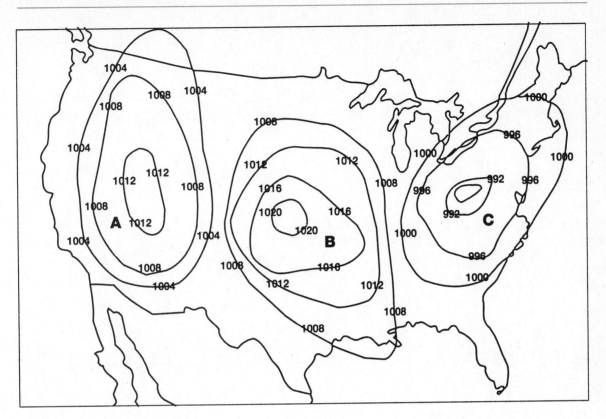

Figure C

Figure C shows three pressure areas, A, B, and C. Study each one. Then answer these questions.

1. Area A is a _____ pressure area.
    <u>high, low</u>

2. The weather in area A is probably _____ .
    <u>fair, cloudy</u>

3. Area B is a _____ pressure area.
    <u>high, low</u>

4. The weather in B probably is _____ .
    <u>fair, cloudy</u>

5. Area C is a _____ pressure area.
    <u>high, low</u>

6. The weather in C probably is _____ .
    <u>fair, cloudy</u>

7. Write the proper symbol in the middle of each pressure area.

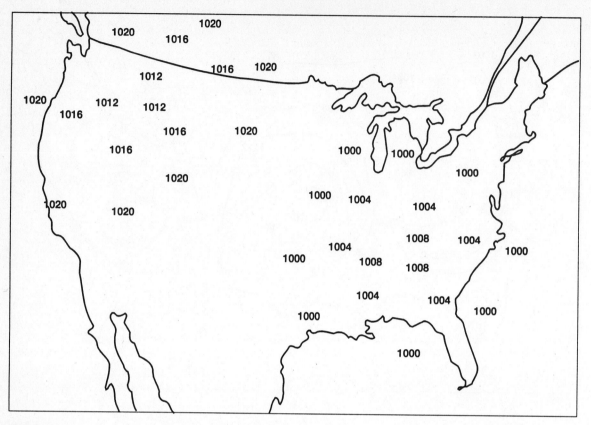

Figure D

Figure D has barometer readings of two pressure areas. One area is in the west. The other is in the east.

Follow the directions. Then fill in the blanks.

1. Study each set of readings. Then draw isobars.

2. Label each pressure area with an H or L.

3. The high-pressure area is in the _____ .
   _{east, west}

4. The low-pressure area is in the _____ .
   _{east, west}

5. The weather in the east is probably _____ .
   _{fair, cloudy}

6. The weather in the west is probably _____ .
   _{fair, cloudy}

How do you read a weather map?

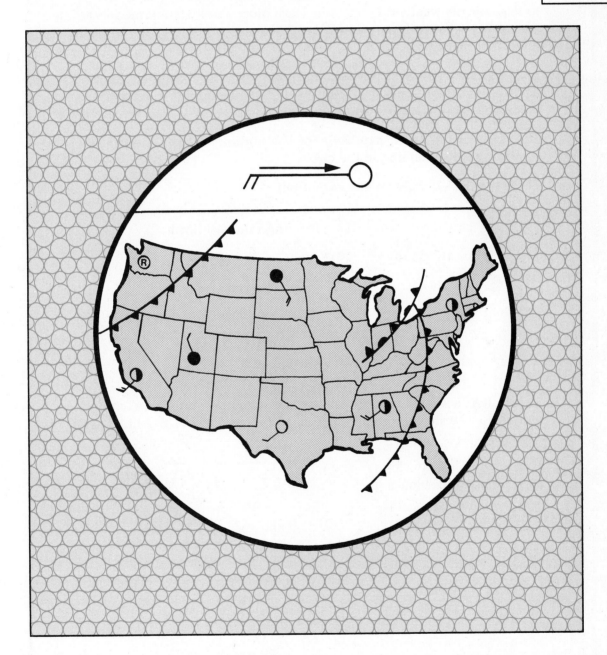

32

LESSON 32 | How do you read a weather map?

In Lesson 30, you learned that weather scientists use <u>station models</u> to show weather conditions. A station model uses symbols instead of words to describe the weather. Now let us learn more about station models so we can see what each part stands for. Then you will know how to read a weather map.

SKY CONDITIONS Each station model is marked by a circle. The circle tells us if the sky is clear, cloudy, or partly cloudy. In most weather maps you see, circles also show precipitation.

The circle of the "clear sky" symbol has nothing on it. All other sky symbols have something in the circle.

These are the symbols for sky conditions:

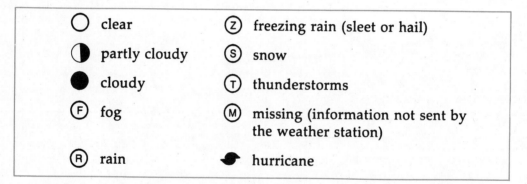

○	clear	Ⓩ	freezing rain (sleet or hail)
◗	partly cloudy	Ⓢ	snow
●	cloudy	Ⓣ	thunderstorms
Ⓕ	fog	Ⓜ	missing (information not sent by the weather station)
Ⓡ	rain	🌀	hurricane

TEMPERATURE It is very easy to show temperature on a station model. Just write the temperature near the city. THAT'S ALL! Easy enough?

This is what "partly cloudy" sky with 20° C temperature looks like:

Figure A

DRAWING CIRCLE SYMBOLS

Draw the circle symbol for each of the following.

	Sky Condition	Symbol			Sky Condition	Symbol
1.	rain			6.	snow	
2.	hail or sleet			7.	hurricane	
3.	information missing			8.	partly cloudy	
4.	fog			9.	thunderstorms	
5.	clear			10.	cloudy	

IDENTIFYING CIRCLE SYMBOLS

What do these symbols mean?

	Symbol	Meaning			Symbol	Meaning
1.	Ⓩ			6.	🌀	
2.	Ⓜ			7.	Ⓕ	
3.	Ⓣ			8.	Ⓡ	
4.	○			9.	◐	
5.	●			10.	Ⓢ	

The weather map (Figure B) shows the sky conditions and temperatures of fifteen cities. Use this weather map to fill in the chart.

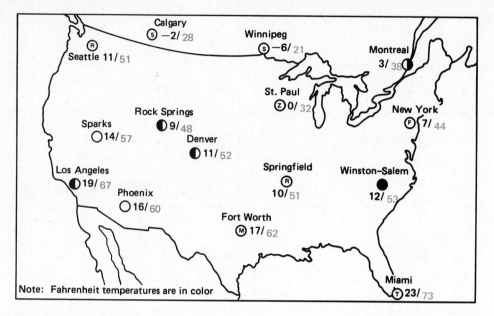

Figure B

	City	Sky Condition	Temperature (° C)
1.	Calgary, Alberta		
2.	Denver, Colorado		
3.	Fort Worth, Texas		
4.	Los Angeles, California		
5.	Miami, Florida		
6.	Montreal, Quebec		
7.	New York, N.Y.		
8.	Phoenix, Arizona		
9.	Rock Springs, Wyoming		
10.	Seattle, Washington		
11.	Sparks, Nevada		
12.	Springfield, Ohio		
13.	St. Paul, Minnesota		
14.	Winnipeg, Manitoba		
15.	Winston-Salem, N.C.		

Wind is an important part of weather. Wind is also an important part of a weather map.

The symbol for wind is a long line with small lines on the end. The small lines are called "feathers" or "flags." There are full flags ‾‾‾‾⌐ and half flags ‾‾‾‾⌐.

A wind symbol tells us two things:

(1) <u>how fast</u> the wind is blowing

(2) the <u>direction</u> it is coming from

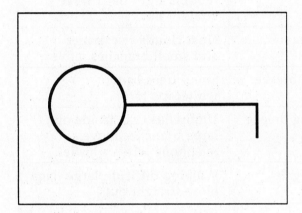

Figure C *Slight breeze*

WIND SPEED The number and length of the flags tell the wind speed. More flags mean faster wind. Fewer flags mean slower wind. For example, the symbol in Figure C shows a slight breeze.

The chart on page 196 shows the rest of the wind speed symbols.

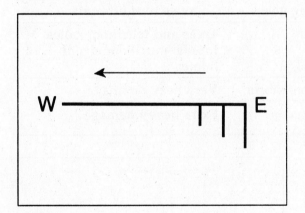

Figure D

WIND DIRECTION Wind direction is shown by an arrow. And we use this fact to tell wind direction—THE ARROW FLIES WITH THE WIND. The arrows point into the direction from which the wind is blowing.

The wind in Figure D is heading west. It is coming from the east. It is called an east wind. (Remember, a wind is named for the direction it comes <u>from</u>.)

WIND CHART

Symbol	Speed miles per hour	km per hour	Description	What The Wind Does
○	less than 1 per hour	less than 2 per hour	calm	Smoke rises straight up
○—	1-3	2-5	light air	Smoke moves with the wind
○—	4-7	6-11	slight breeze	Face feels wind; leaves rustle; flags stir
○—	8-12	12-19	gentle breeze	Leaves and twigs in constant motion; light flags wave straight out
○—	13-18	20-29	moderate breeze	Dust clouds rise; paper and small branches move
○—	19-24	30-39	fresh breeze	Small trees bend; whitecaps form
○—	25-31	40-50	strong breeze	Umbrellas turn inside out; large branches move; telephone wires whistle
○—	32-38	51-61	near gale	Walking difficult; large flags blow straight out
○—	39-46	62-74	gale	Walking is extra difficult; twigs break off trees
○—	47-54	75-87	strong gale	Shingles torn off roofs
○—	55-63	88-101	storm	Trees and telephone poles topple; much damage to homes
○—	64-75	102-120	violent storm	Very heavy damage
○—	over 75	over 120	hurricane	Extra heavy damage

Measuring wind was first done by sailors on ships. They used different flags to show how strong the wind was blowing.

Now these symbols are used by the Weather Service to show wind on a map.

What is the strongest wind you have ever felt? Answer by drawing the symbol in the box.

COMPLETE THE CHART

Study the ten symbols shown below. Then fill in the missing information on the chart. The first one has been completed for you.

	Wind Symbol	Speed (kilometers per hour)	Description	Name
1.		20-29	moderate breeze	east wind
2.	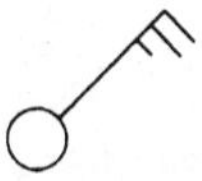			
3.				
4.				
5.				
6.				
7.				
8.				
9.				
10.	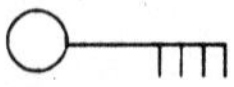			

Study the symbols on the weather map (Figure E). Then fill in the chart.

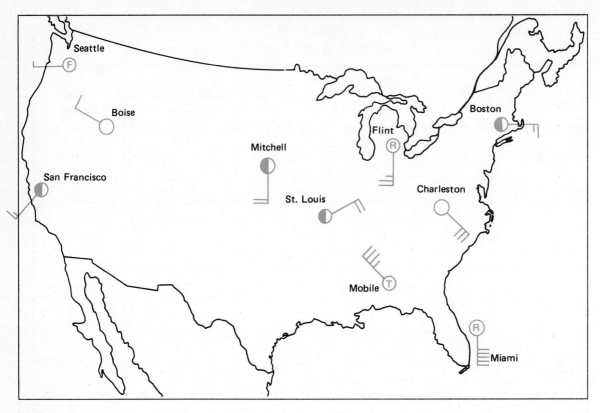

Figure E

	City	Sky Condition	Wind Speed (kph)	Wind Coming From	Wind Heading Towards
1.	Boise, Idaho				
2.	Boston, Mass.				
3.	Charleston, W. V.				
4.	Flint, Mich.				
5.	Miami, Fla.				
6.	Mitchell, S.D.				
7.	Mobile, Ala.				
8.	San Francisco, Calif.				
9.	Seattle, Wash.				
10.	St. Louis, Mo.				

THE METRIC SYSTEM

METRIC-ENGLISH CONVERSIONS

	Metric to English	English to Metric
Length	1 kilometer = 0.621 mile (mi)	1 mi = 1.61 km
	1 meter = 3.28 feet (ft)	1 ft = 0.305 m
	1 centimeter = 0.394 inch (in)	1 in = 2.54 cm
Area	1 square meter = 10.763 square feet	1 ft^2 = 0.0929 m^2
	1 square centimeter = 0.155 square inch	1 in^2 = 6.452 cm^2
Volume	1 cubic meter = 35.315 cubic feet	1 ft^3 = 0.0283 m^3
	1 cubic centimeter = 0.0610 cubic inches	1 in^3 = 16.39 cm^3
	1 liter = .2642 gallon (gal)	1 gal = 3.79 L
	1 liter = 1.06 quart (qt)	1 qt = 0.94 L
Mass	1 kilogram = 2.205 pound (lb)	1 lb = 0.4536 kg
	1 gram = 0.0353 ounce (oz)	1 oz = 28.35 g
Temperature	Celsius = 5/9 (°F –32)	Fahrenheit = 9/5°C + 32
	0°C = 32°F (Freezing point of water)	72°F = 22°C (Room temperature)
	100°C = 212°F	98.6°F = 37°C
	(Boiling point of water)	(Human body temperature)

METRIC UNITS

The basic unit is printed in capital letters.

Length	Symbol
Kilometer	km
METER	m
centimeter	cm
millimeter	mm

Area	Symbol
square kilometer	km^2
SQUARE METER	m^2
square millimeter	mm^2

Volume	Symbol
CUBIC METER	m^3
cubic millimeter	mm^3
liter	L
milliliter	mL

Mass	Symbol
KILOGRAM	kg
gram	g

Temperature	Symbol
degree Celsius	°C

SOME COMMON METRIC PREFIXES

Prefix		Meaning
micro-	=	0.000001, or 1/1,000,000
milli-	=	0.001, or 1/1000
centi-	=	0.01, or 1/100
deci-	=	0.1, or 1/10
deka-	=	10
hecto-	=	100
kilo-	=	1000
mega-	=	1,000,000

SOME METRIC RELATIONSHIPS

Unit	Relationship
kilometer	1 km = 1000 m
meter	1 m = 100 cm
centimeter	1 cm = 10 mm
millimeter	1mm = 0.1 cm
liter	1 L = 1000 mL
milliliter	1 mL = 0.001 L
tonne	1 t = 1000 kg
kilogram	1 kg = 1000 g
gram	1 g = 1000 mg
centigram	1 cg = 10 mg
milligram	1 mg = 0.001 g

GLOSSARY/INDEX

air currents [KUR-unts]: up and down movements of air, 94

air mass: large area of air that has the same temperature and amount of moisture, 158

anemometer [an-uh-MOM-uh-tur]: instrument used to measure wind speed, 86

atmosphere [AT-mus-feer]: envelope of gases that surrounds the earth, 44

barometer [buh-ROM-uh-ter]: instrument used to measure air pressure, 82

cirrus [SIR-us]: light, feathery clouds, 138

cold front: forward edge of a cold air mass, formed when a cold air mass pushes under a warm air mass, 168

condensation [kahn-dun-SAY-shun]: changing of a gas to a liquid, 132

conduction [kon-DUCK-shun]: movement of heat through a solid, 68

continental [KAHNT-un-ent-ul] **air mass:** air mass that forms over land, 158

continental shelf: part of a continent that slopes gently away from the shoreline, 26

continental slope: part of a continent between the continental shelf and the ocean floor, 26

convection [kon-VEK-shun]: movement of heat through a liquid or a gas, 68

crest: highest point of a wave, 20

cumulus [KYOOM-yuh-lus]: big, puffy clouds, 138

dew point: temperature to which air must be cooled to reach saturation, 132

front: surface between different air masses, 162

ground water: water that collects in pores in the soil, 8

hurricane [hur-uh-KAYN]: tropical storm with very strong winds, 174

hydrosphere [HY-droh-sfeer]: water part of our planet, 2

ionosphere [Y-on-uh-sferr]: upper layer of the atmosphere, 62

isobar [Y-suh-bar]: line on a weather map that connects points of equal pressure, 186

land breeze: breeze coming from the land toward the sea, 100

maritime [MAR-ih-tym] **air mass:** air mass that forms over oceans, 158

meteorologist [meet-ee-uhr-AHL-uh-jist]: person who studies weather, 180

mid-ocean ridge: underwater mountain range, 26

millibars [MIL-uh-bahrz]: unit of measurement for air pressure, 186

mountain breeze: cool air that moves down from a mountain, 108

oceanography [oh-shun-OG-ruh-fee]: study of the oceans, 15

ocean currents: streams of water flowing in oceans, 2

phytoplankton [fite-uh-PLANK-tun]: floating plants, 32

polar air mass: air mass that forms over cold regions, 158

precipitation [prih-sip-uh-TAY-shun]: water that falls to the earth from the atmosphere, 144

properties [PROP-ur-tees]: characteristics used to describe an object, 50

psychrometer [sy-KRAHM-uh-tur]: instrument that measures relative humidity, 126

radiation [ray-dee-AY-shun]: movement of energy through empty space, 68

rain gauge [GAYJ]: instrument used to measure precipitation, 146

relative humidity [hyoo-MID-uh-tee]: amount of water vapor in the air compared to the amount of water vapor the air can hold, 120

respiration [res-puh-RAY-shun]: process by which living things combine food and oxygen to get energy, 44

sea breeze: breeze coming from the sea towards the land, 100

station model: record of weather information at a weather station, 182

stationary [STAY-shuh-ner-ee] **front:** boundary between two unlike air masses where there is little movement of air, 168

stratosphere [STRAT-uh-sfeer]: middle layer of the atmosphere, 62

stratus [STRAT-us]: clouds that form layers across the sky, 138

submersibles [sub-MUR-suh-bulz]: underwater research vessel, 14

thunderstorm: storm with thunder, lightening, heavy rain, and strong winds, 174

tornado [tohr-NAY-doh]: small, very violent funnel-shaped storm, 174

tropical [TRAHP-ih-kul] **air mass:** air mass that forms over warm regions, 158

troposphere [TROHP-uh-sfeer]: lowest layer of the atmosphere, 62

trough [TROFF]: lowest point of a wave, 20

valley breeze: cool air that moves up from a valley, 108

warm front: forward edge of a warm air mass formed when a warm air mass pushes over a cold air mass, 162

water vapor: water in the gas form found in air, 120

wave: regular up-and-down movement of water, 20

wavelength: distance from one crest to the next crest, 20

weather: day to day conditions of the atmosphere, 114

wind: horizontal movement of air, 86

wind vane: instrument used to measure wind direction, 86